# PRAYERS FOR CLEANSING ANCESTRAL BLOODLINES
## IN THE
# COURTS OF HEAVEN

---

SECOND EDITION

"WHOEVER CONCEALS THEIR
SINS DOES NOT PROSPER, BUT
THE ONE WHO CONFESSES AND
RENOUNCES THEM FINDS MERCY."

– PROVERBS 28:13 (NIV)

# PRAYERS FOR CLEANSING ANCESTRAL BLOODLINES IN THE COURTS OF HEAVEN

FOR FAMILIES, INDIVIDUALS, COUPLES, ORGANIZATIONS, CITIES, COUNTIES, STATES, REGIONS & NATIONS

## DR. BRUCE COOK

TERRITORIAL DIRECTOR FOR ROBERT HENDERSON

KINGDOM HOUSE PUBLISHING | LAKEBAY WASHINGTON

iv

PRAYERS FOR CLEANSING ANCESTRAL BLOODLINES
IN THE COURTS OF HEAVEN—SECOND EDITION
For Families, Individuals, Couples, Organizations, Cities, Counties, States, Regions & Nations
Copyright © 2017, 2020, 2021, 2024 by Dr. Bruce Cook

All rights reserved. This publication may not be reproduced, stored in a retrieval system, or transmitted in any form or by any means—electronic, mechanical, photocopy, recording, scanning, or other—without prior, written permission of the author. You may use brief excerpts from this resource for the purpose of presentations, articles, or a brief quotation in a book. The author guarantees all contents are original and do not infringe upon the legal rights of any other person or work.

Published by Kingdom House Publishing, Lakebay, Washington.

Printed in the United States of America.

Initial Release, January 2021. Second Edition, September 2024.

Layout and formatting by Wendy K. Walters. www.wendykwalters.com

ISBN (print media): 978-1-939944-53-5

ISBN (ePub): 978-1-939944-54-2

ISBN (Kindle): 978-1-939944-55-9

LCCN: 2020911629

Scripture Versions Used in This Work:

Portions of scripture taken from the Amplified © Bible are marked AMP. Copyright © 1954, 1958, 1962, 1964, 1965, 1987 by The Lockman Foundation. Used by permission. www.lockman.org

Portions of scripture taken from the Berean Study Bible are marked BSB. The Holy Bible, Berean Study Bible, BSB. Copyright © 2016, 2018 by Bible Hub. Used by Permission. All Rights Reserved Worldwide.

Scripture quotations marked CSB are taken from the Christian Standard Bible ©, Copyright Verdana 2017 by Holman Bible Publishers. Used by permission. Christian Standard Bible•, and CSBVerdana are federally registered trademarks of Holman Bible Publishers.

Portions of scripture taken from the English Standard Version are marked ESV. Copyright © 2001 by Crossway Bibles, a division of Good News Publishers. Used by permission. All rights reserved.

Scriptures marked as "(GNT)" are taken from the Good News Translation - Second Edition © 1992 by American Bible Society. Used by permission.

Portions of scripture taken from God's Word Translation are marked GW. GOD'S WORD is a copyrighted work of God's Word to the Nations Bible Society. Quotations are used by permission. Copyright © 1995 by God's Word to the Nations. All rights reserved.

Portions of scripture taken from the Holman Christian Standard Bible are marked HCS. Copyright © 1999, 2000, 2002, 2003 by Holman Bible Publishers. All rights reserved.

Portions of scripture taken from the King James Version are marked KJV. Originally published in 1611, this Bible is in the public domain.

Portions of scripture taken from the THE MESSAGE are marked MSG. by Eugene H. Peterson. Copyright © 1993, 1994, 1995, 1996, 2000, 2001, 2002. Used by permission of NavPress Publishing Group.

Portions of scripture taken from the New American Standard Bible are marked NASB. Copyright © 1960, 1962, 1963, 1968, 1971, 1972, 1973,1975, 1977, 1995 by The Lockman Foundation. Used by permission.

Portions of scripture taken from the Holy Bible, New International Version ©, NIV © are marked NIV. Copyright © 1973, 1978, 1984 by the International Bible Society. Used by permission of Zondervan Publishing House. All rights reserved. The "NIV" and "New International Version" are trademarks registered in the United States Patent and Trademark Office by the International Bible Society. Use of either trademark requires the permission of the International Bible Society.

Portions of scripture taken from the New King James Version are marked NKJV. Copyright © 1979, 1980, 1982 by Thomas Nelson, Inc. Used by permission. All rights reserved.

Portions of scripture taken from The Holy Bible, New Living Translation are marked NLT. Copyright © 1996. Used by permission by Tyndale House Publishers, Inc., Wheaton, IL. All rights reserved.

Scripture quotations marked TPT are from The Passion Translation ©. Copyright © 2017, 2018 by Passion & Fire Ministries, Inc. Used by permission. All rights reserved. ThePassionTranslation.com.

Portions of the Epilogue dealing with stewardship are co-authored with Lynn Hare and adapted from Chapter 19 of *The 8th Mountain*, by Dr. Bruce Cook (2017), Lakebay, WA: Kingdom House Publishing.

Several definitions contained herein are taken from Wikipedia and are used by permission. https://creativecommons.org/licenses/by-sa/3.0/ The Wikimedia Foundation, Inc. is a nonprofit charitable organization dedicated to encouraging the growth, development and distribution of free, multilingual content, and to providing the full content of these wiki-based projects to the public free of charge. The Wikimedia Foundation provides the essential infrastructure for free knowledge, and hosts Wikipedia, the free online encyclopedia, created, edited, and verified by volunteers around the world, as well as many other vital community projects. Wikipedia is a free encyclopedia written in 300 languages by volunteers around the world. Wikipedia needs knowledge from all languages and cultures. Wikipedia welcomes others who share its vision, and invites them to join in collecting and sharing knowledge that fully represents human diversity.

TO CONTACT THE AUTHOR:
brucecook77@gmail.com
THECOURTSOFHEAVEN.ORG

"SETTLE MATTERS QUICKLY WITH YOUR ADVERSARY WHO IS TAKING YOU TO COURT. DO IT WHILE YOU ARE STILL TOGETHER ON THE WAY, OR YOUR ADVERSARY MAY HAND YOU OVER TO THE JUDGE, AND THE JUDGE MAY HAND YOU OVER TO THE OFFICER, AND YOU MAY BE THROWN INTO PRISON."

– MATTHEW 5:25 (NIV)

# ACKNOWLEDGMENTS

Thank you to the Holy Spirit for releasing this revelation for such a time as this. The Holy Spirit leads and guides us into all the truth as we follow His leading and prompting and still, small voice (John 16:13).

Special thanks to Robert Henderson for mentoring me in the Courts of Heaven, and for introducing me to his global network of Hub Leaders, Continental Directors, Territorial (Regional) Directors, and State Directors. They are a special group of people and anointed ministers and leaders who are called by God and love to serve others.

Also, my personal thanks and gratitude to Elizabeth Sorensen and Edie Glaser, who helped me proofread and edit the manuscript and did an amazing, excellent job. You have keen vision and sharp, eagle eyes. The final product is greatly improved because of your efforts.

As always, Wendy Walters is a consummate pro and makes everything look and read better. Her designs shine and sparkle with the light and glory of God, and are elegant and anointed. She has earned her nickname of Wendy "Wow" Walters over the years on multiple projects we have done together, including this one. Thank you!

I also extend a special thanks to my Courts of Heaven teammates, great friends and spiritual mentors, Mark and Suzi Henderson, for your love, support and friendship through the years. It's been a great ride so far and it's not over yet. The best is yet to come. And thanks also to our newest team members, Denny and Estelle Blewett. You are a blessing!

I also express heartfelt thanks to Dennis Wiedrick for his friendship, encouragement, and spiritual mentoring; for writing the terrific Foreword and for sharing several helpful comments on the manuscript.

I saved the best for last—thank you, Caroline, my wonderful wife. You exhibited extraordinary grace and patience with me during the many long hours of researching, writing and editing this book. I love you, sweetheart, and many thanks for your love, support and prayers.

"IF YOU FORGIVE THE
SINS OF ANY, THEY ARE
FORGIVEN THEM; IF YOU
RETAIN THE SINS OF ANY,
THEY ARE RETAINED."

– JOHN 20:23 (NKJV)

# DEDICATION

To the Hendersons—
Robert and Mary, Mark and Suzi.

Thank you for speaking and sowing into my life
and into the lives of many others globally.

"IF WE CONFESS OUR SINS, HE IS
FAITHFUL AND JUST TO FORGIVE
US OUR SINS AND TO CLEANSE US
FROM ALL UNRIGHTEOUSNESS."

– 1 JOHN 1:9 (NKJV, BSB)

# CONTENTS

xiii ENDORSEMENTS

xxiii PREFACE

xxix FOREWORD BY DENNIS WIEDRICK

1 PART ONE ·····································
PREPARING AND PRESENTING YOUR
CASE IN THE COURTS OF HEAVEN

3 CHAPTER 1
FAMILIES AND ANCESTRAL BLOODLINES

23 CHAPTER 2
PREPARING TO ENTER THE COURTS OF HEAVEN

49 CHAPTER 3
ENTERING THE COURTS OF HEAVEN

75 CHAPTER 4
PRESENTING, REVIEWING AND WEIGHING
THE EVIDENCE IN YOUR CASE

95 PART TWO ·····································
PRAYER TEMPLATES FOR THE 10 CORE AREAS
OF ANCESTRAL BLOODLINE REPENTANCE

97 CHAPTER 5
SETTING THE STAGE FOR REPENTANCE

107 CHAPTER 6
IDOLATRY AND FALSE GODS

117 CHAPTER 7
FREEMASONRY AND SECRET SOCIETIES

133 CHAPTER 8
OCCULT AND WITCHCRAFT

141 CHAPTER 9
SEXUAL SINS

149 CHAPTER 10
INNOCENT BLOODSHED AND
ACTS OF VIOLENCE

xii |

155     CHAPTER 11
FINANCIAL SINS AND MAMMON

165     CHAPTER 12
ADDICTIONS AND DYSFUNCTIONS

175     CHAPTER 13
RELIGION

181     CHAPTER 14
RACIAL, GENDER, AGE AND CULTURAL
BIAS, PREJUDICE, DISCRIMINATION
AND PERSECUTION

187     CHAPTER 15
SINS OF OMISSION

193     PART THREE·······································
RESTING YOUR CASE AND RECEIVING
AND ENFORCING YOUR VERDICT

195     CHAPTER 16
RESTING YOUR CASE AND
RECEIVING YOUR VERDICT

205     CHAPTER 17
WALKING OUT AND ENFORCING
YOUR VERDICT

213     CHAPTER 18
ONGOING MAINTENANCE AND REPENTANCE
FOR ANY NEW ISSUES THAT MAY ARISE

217     CHAPTER 19
PRAYING FOR ORGANIZATIONS, CITIES,
COUNTIES, STATES, REGIONS AND NATIONS

237     EPILOGUE

245     APPENDIX A
QUESTIONS AND ANSWERS

249     APPENDIX B
DECLARATIONS AND DECREES OF REPENTANCE

# ENDORSEMENTS

Over the past few years many of us, even we who have no legal background, have become familiar with the legal terminology used in courts of law and criminal cases. This is as a direct result of 24/7 news channels or even popular TV shows. This exciting book takes our understanding of our legal authority into the spiritual realm, and it identifies and confirms the authority that we have as Christ believers and equips us with the tools required to further expand and multiply repentance by the global body of Christ.

As believers, we have both a mandate and responsibility to represent our families, cities and even our nations before the King of kings in the Courts of Heaven. We can usher in God's kingdom on earth as we represent and then repent for current and generational sins in our family lines or in our communities. As our understanding grows regarding our legal status in the Courts of Heaven, we will be emboldened to take on the most "difficult cases" because we know without a shadow of doubt who represents us in the Heavenlies. It is Jesus! As we operate in this truth, we will have an even greater influence into every sphere of cultural influence.

I gladly endorse this inspiring book.

GRAHAM POWER
Chairman, Power Group
www.powergrp.co.za
Founder of the Global Day of Prayer and Unashamedly Ethical
www.globalvoiceofprayer.com
www.unashamedlyethical.com
Blackheath, Cape Town, South Africa
Author: *Not By Might Nor By Power*

Since the time the Philippian jailor cried out, "What must I do?", we as leaders have been called to give concrete instruction and guidance to the world. This is exactly what Dr. Bruce Cook has done here. Based on years of revelation, confirmed by thousands of hours in putting these principles into practice, and the testimonies of countless successes, we can now say we have a prophetic roadmap for how we can lead God's people out of all bondages and curses that have been passed down through our bloodlines. This book marks a true Blood Line drawn in the sand of Satan's plots and schemes against us. Come on, Church, let's rise up and "Let my people go!"

KEVIN GRAVES
Founder and President
Target Ministries
Singapore, Singapore

Your legal rights in the kingdom of God are an essential baseline. Unfortunately, so many of us are fighting the wrong fight. Enter the Courts of Heaven and litigate your case! Dr. Cook has been a friend and trusted advisor for many years. I have personally experienced the impact and freedom from this COH process. This critical work is a game changer for the millions of Christ followers who need freedom. Right now! We have rights and privileges as kingdom kids. We have an Advocate, Jesus, who is ready to set it straight. Let's do our part, understand our rights and exercise them. This handbook will help you to understand kingdom law and exercise your inherited positional rights. Dr. Cook once again shapes a complex subject into an everyday useful tool. The verdict is yours—it is finished!

DOUG SPADA
Founder & President, WorkLife Inc
www.worklife.org
Principal, Espada Ventures LLC
Cumming, Georgia
Author: *Monday Morning Atheist*

Not many know their way around the heavenly Courtroom with the skill, discernment and God-given authority to legislate there like Dr. Bruce Cook. I've witnessed two separate sessions he led; both were life changing. Going to the Courts of Heaven is a journey the enemy does not want you to make, for he knows he will be defeated. The Courts are where you will be heard—and where you will be granted the freedom you have longed for to fulfill your destiny.

Dr. Bruce writes, "Someone, sometime, somewhere, needs to stand in the gap and pray the prayers of repentance for your ancestral bloodline." Let that someone be you ... there are few callings more noble than this one!

CANDACE L. LONG
Teacher • Author • Coach
Founder, auDEO Media Group
www.candacelong.com
Jasper, Georgia
Author: *The Levitical Calling, Letters to Aleeyah:*
*A Personal Journey of Generational Healing,*
*The Ancient Path to Creativity and Innovation*

Dr. Bruce Cook's new book, *Prayers for Cleansing Ancestral Bloodlines in the Courts of Heaven*, is a powerful guide on how you can cleanse your ancestral bloodline. It not only includes valuable teaching but also provides practical step-by-step prayer templates. For those who seek to gain understanding and helpful application on cleansing your ancestral bloodline, please consider reading Dr. Cook's excellent book. I have prayed these prayers myself and can attest that they are effective and powerful!

CHRISTINE CHEN
President & Director
Elohim International Limited Company
Wonderful Prosperity Limited Company
Car League
Kaohsiung City, Taiwan

Whenever new understandings in the Body of Christ begin to emerge, they are generally spearheaded by experience. At some point a scholarly but spiritual guidebook needs to be written to define terms, lay down procedures, outline protocol and articulate in a meaningful way, the value of the experience. This is what Dr. Bruce Cook has done with this "Courts of Heaven" book. He has described our access into this heavenly place so clearly and in such a nonthreatening way, that ordinary people, through reading these pages, will be able to appropriate the experience. Thank you Dr. Bruce for this labor of love that will help many believers worldwide to grasp how to cleanse and break the chains of ancestral bloodlines. This will prayerfully give them the ability to serve Christ in a deeper, cleaner and more effective way.

DR. BERIN GILFILLAN
Founder & CEO
Good Shepherd Ministries International
International School of Ministry (ISOM)
San Bernardino, California
Author: *Pursuing Maturity: The Goal of God, and Unlocking*
*The Abraham Promise: Mobilize to Multiply*

This book is very thorough, well written and documented. Dr. Bruce Cook unpacks the judicial process to empower believers to experience breakthrough, healing, and deliverance by often overlooked areas that can cause havoc in one's life. *Prayers for Cleansing Ancestral Bloodlines in the Courts of Heaven* comprehensively addresses and unveils some of Satan's dark secrets that often hold believers in captivity, and provides a clear pathway to freedom. Throughout the book, biblical precedence is set and the steps are clearly defined along with powerful prayers to bring people into the victorious life. The application of this process can be extended beyond the individual to families, communities, organizations, businesses, and nations as well to bring greater freedom.

If you need a strong foundation and guide in understanding the Courts of Heaven and what your rights are with all the terms clearly defined, this is the book for you! It is a blueprint you can follow to gain greater breakthrough and freedom. I know this to be true because I have prayed these prayers myself and found that they work!

WILL MEIER
Project Engineering Discipline Manager – Fortune 50 Aerospace Company
Founder of Awakening Destiny Global – www.awakeningdestiny.global
Founder of Coaching for Impact – www. coaching4impact.com
Manchester, Connecticut
Author of *Leaders for Life – Creating Champions through the
NOW Leadership Process* – www.leadersforlife.global


*Prayers for Cleansing Ancestral Bloodlines in the Courts of Heaven* is the most detailed book I have ever read on the subject of operating in the Courts of Heaven and contains a divine blueprint for cleansing ancestral bloodlines from the Courts of Heaven. The book leaves no stone unturned as it attempts to bring a final solution to Satan's malicious attempts to arrest our destinies by bringing accusations against us in the Courts of Heaven because of iniquities and transgressions attached to our not so perfect ancestral bloodlines.

This book provides both the protocols and prayers for winning cases against our bloodlines in the Courts of Heaven. I highly recommend this thorough and scholastic treatise on this most important revelation of our time. I promise you that as you read it and pray the prayers, by the end of this book, evil altars Satan has planted in your generational bloodlines, will be destroyed!

DR. FRANCIS MYLES
Founder and President
Francis Myles Global Ministries
Atlanta, Georgia
Author: *Issuing Divine Restraining Orders from the Courts of Heaven*

This book is beautifully written—filled with meat and content that inspires frequent, selah-filled moments of reflection and revelation. Truly, as we live through these days, I'm realizing again and again what a "now" thing your book is. How exciting for you to have such a "catch and release" experience at the highest level! Every time you pick up your pen it's a purpose-filled journey prompted by the Holy Spirit that lands on a destination called "for such a time as this."

- You're a bushwhacker for the Body of Christ, paving the way for "7-Mountain" change makers to accomplish the plans and purposes connected to one's assignments for the season.

- There's a pattern to the way God uses you in YOUR assignment. Each body of work captures the NOW of what the Holy Spirit is doing while you deliver the HOW.

- ... All resulting in personalized, customized blueprints for assignments and destiny!

SHER VALENZUELA
Co-founder & Vice President
First State Manufacturing
www.firststatemfg.com
Milford, Delaware
Author: *The World's Greatest Customer*

After reading the manuscript, I'm convinced that this book is going to have great impact on the lives of those who read it. Congratulations!

DR. ARLEEN WESTERHOF
Director, Center for Economics and Mutuality
www.eom.org
Founder and Executive Director, European Economic Summit
www.economicsummit.eu
Amsterdam, The Netherlands

The Church, God's people, is now passing over into a new unfolding era of Isaiah 2:1-5 and Micah 4:1-5, which are known as the "mountain of the Lord's house." I believe this will be the greatest move of God in human history and usher in the great end-time harvest. As it was vital in the first Passover era, so it is now vital in today's passing over, that the chains and remembrances of past and present bondage to sin, i.e., all leaven—every contaminant, hindrance, and limitation—be removed from your house, wherein His Holy Spirit dwells, in preparation for the Passover seder, the great marriage supper of the Lamb.

This eye-opening, timely book, details the length, breadth, height, and depth of God's love and power to save (cleanse) to the uttermost. Meet in God's Court and let your house be cleansed from every bondage, sin effect, and limitation. Pass over into the new era! Court awaits! Revelation awaits! Pass over! This is an amazing work! The topic is exhaustively scrutinized and explained in clear language. Most timely indeed. I have personally benefited from these prayers and so can you. Great job—phenomenal work!

DR. ERIK A. KUDLIS
Author, Speaker, Statesman, CEO and International Businessman
Go Modular, Ltd.
www.go-modular.co.uk
Erik's Design & Build Associates, Inc.
www.edbhomes.com
Jewett City, Connecticut

Throughout my years of ministry, I have discovered that there are believers in the world today that are not only fearful when entering the throne room of God, but are insecure while presenting their supplications to our Heavenly Father.

Thank God for Dr. Bruce Cook and this Holy Spirit-inspired book. I believe this will help every believer to not only present their supplications, but will also give them the courage and the strength and the power to defeat the Devil.

DR. JESS BIELBY
www.jessbielby.org
Founder and President
Gospel Associates
Kingdom Prophetics
www.kingdomprophetics.com
Benton, Kansas

As I read *Prayers for Cleansing Ancestral Bloodlines in the Courts of Heaven*, the following Scripture came to mind: *"Therefore, my dear friends, as you have always obeyed, not only in my presence, but now how much more in my absence, continue to work out your Salvation with fear and trembling, for it is God who works in you to will and to act in order to fulfill his good purpose"* (Phil. 2:12-13).

You have been handed a powerful tool through the work of Dr. Bruce Cook in this book. This work by Dr. Cook has provided you a systematic and thorough process of being able to accomplish the "working out of my salvation with fear and trembling." Dr. Cook's work in this book is a comprehensive, clear, concise instruction manual, biblically-based, in which he lays out a step-by-step approach in which you can examine, with the help of the Holy Spirit, your life and ancestral bloodlines for unrepented sin.

You are then given a clear and thorough process for repenting of those sins and taking your case before our Heavenly

Father, the Just Judge, the One Who Judges Righteously, whose very foundation of His throne is righteousness and justice, and through the finished work of Christ Jesus on the cross. He faithfully and mercifully grants us forgiveness and answers to our prayers.

As you read this book, expect to grow and mature in your prayer life as you apply the instructions and you do the work of "working out your salvation with fear and trembling." My life has been deeply changed and enriched by the treasure contained in this book. Thank you, Dr. Cook, for pouring all that you have poured into this book. I have received such a rich, full and continuing blessing from it. May all who read this book be forever changed by the Spirit of God at work in their lives through the instruction, knowledge and process you have shared with us in *Prayers for Cleansing Ancestral Bloodlines in the Courts of Heaven*.

ELIZABETH SORENSEN
State Director, Washington Prayer Caucus Network
Pastor, Christian Life Missions, Deborah Team
Minister with the Full Gospel Fellowship of Churches and Ministries International
Orting, Washington


This is a great book that is loaded with solid revelation and a lot of research. Bruce Cook has carefully laid out a compelling case for ancestral bloodline cleansing that is appropriate for us to present before the Courts of Heaven. It has opened my eyes to another realm of prayer and I know it will do the same for you.

PAUL L. CUNY
Founder and President
MarketPlace Leadership International
www.marketplaceleadership.com
Jacksonville, Florida
Author of *Nehemiah People* and *Secrets of the Kingdom Economy*

*Prayers for Cleansing Ancestral Bloodlines in the Courts of Heaven* shares some very deep insight into the protocols of kingdom concepts that are largely foreign in the body of Christ today. As the Church grows in its perceptions and knowledge of these concepts, the saints can enter the throne room of God and the Courts of Heaven. It is when Scripture is applied to the need and knowledge of the people, that we have access to the justice of God. This book by Dr. Bruce Cook will challenge you and help transform you into having a mindset of kingdom concepts that are needed widely today!

DR. THERESA PHILLIPS
The King's Ambassador
Founder and President of Destiny Arising
Founder and President of Global Prophetic Voice
Bishop and Senior Pastor
Kingdom Global Impact Center
www.destinyarising.net
www.globalpropheticvoice.com
www.DrTheresaPhillips.com
St. Charles, Illinois

In Bruce Cook's book, *Prayers for Cleansing Ancestral Bloodlines in the Courts of Heaven*, he carefully leads us in understanding an important truth and tool, Courtroom prayer. Particularly helpful in the book are the sample prayers. They skillfully lead and model prayers to assist your time in prayer. Bruce is equipping the saints for the work of service. By choosing to journey with him and the Holy Spirit on this walk, it will open you to important truths to equip you in your work of service to the King of kings and His kingdom.

AL CAPERNA
Founder and Chairman
CMC Group
www.cmcgp.com
Bowling Green, Ohio

# PREFACE

I have endeavored to write a handbook that will help to bring structure and definition and provide a protocol, process and prayer templates for the Courts of Heaven, and in doing so, to make it more readily accessible, available, applicable and practical to the body of Christ globally. I am indebted to those who have preceded me and have pioneered this emerging area of theology and avenue of Courtroom prayer, especially Robert Henderson. I write from the perspective of both a practitioner and a theologian, a social scientist and an ordained minister, as well as a business and political leader, and someone who is part of the leadership team of a local church, a director of several other ministries, and has co-founded and led an apostolic network.

I have analyzed and reported what I have seen to work in the field, in actual practice, as someone who is a Magistrate and Navigator in the Courts of Heaven, and who has led well over 2,500 sessions for several thousand people to date in some 25-30 nations.

My research and findings build upon the growing body of literature in this field and on this subject, and I believe they are synergistic and complementary to the work of others, and add new insights, revelation, and perspective while staying true to the strong foundation that has already been laid by Robert Henderson and others. If I can point people to Jesus, and shine a light upon His ongoing work and crucial roles in heaven as Advocate, Mediator, and High Priest for the saints and body of Christ while we are on earth, I will have been successful in large measure.

While much more than that is addressed in these pages— including a legal and spiritual framework and foundation for the Courts of Heaven—my focus is on Christ, His blood and righteousness, His finished work at the cross, His ongoing work in heaven, and what that means for you and your family both on earth and in the Courts of Heaven. This will become abundantly clear as you continue to read and unpack each of the chapters which follow and pray the prayers of repentance.

Jesus is pre-eminently qualified to represent you in the Courts of Heaven as your Advocate. His track record is unmatched, unequalled, unparalleled and unblemished. He has extensive firsthand experience with Satan, the archenemy of your soul, and He alone defeated death, plundered hell, and brought back the keys of death, hell and the grave. Jesus suffered rejection, betrayal, mocking, abandonment, and more—being sold for 30 pieces of silver, beatings, scourging, flogging, whipping, having a crown of thorns placed on his head, having soldiers cast lots for His linen tunic, and being stripped naked in public and nailed to a cross to die an agonizing death while onlookers reviled, mocked, jeered, ridiculed, cursed and insulted Him. He understands pain, suffering and trauma all too well, and can empathize with you.

Isa. 53:3 (ESV) says, *"He was despised and rejected by men, a man of sorrows and acquainted with grief; and as one from whom men hide their faces he was despised, and we esteemed him not."* The TPT adds, *"He was despised and rejected by men, a man of deep sorrows who was no stranger to suffering and grief. We hid our faces from him in disgust and considered him a nobody, not worthy of respect."* And God's Word translation states, *"He was despised and rejected by people. He was a man of sorrows, familiar with suffering. He was despised like one from whom people turn their faces, and we didn't consider him to be worth anything."*

Yet, despite this horrible mistreatment by others, Scripture says that Jesus saw and understood the bigger picture, was able to keep that in mind, and was willing to be obedient to the point of death. Phil. 2:8 (NIV) says, *"And being found in appearance as a man, he humbled himself by becoming obedient to death—even death on a cross!"* Heb. 12:2 (BSB) states, *"Let us fix our eyes on Jesus, the author and perfecter of our faith, who for the joy set before Him endured the cross, scorning its shame, and sat down at the right hand of the throne of God."* The NLT adds, *"We do this by keeping our eyes on Jesus, the champion who initiates and perfects our faith. Because of the joy awaiting him, he endured the cross, disregarding its shame. Now he is seated in the place of honor beside God's throne."*

The Good News Translation notes, *"Let us keep our eyes fixed on Jesus, on whom our faith depends from beginning to end. He did not give up because of the cross! On the contrary, because of the joy that was waiting for him, he thought nothing of the disgrace of dying on the cross, and he is now seated at the right side of God's throne."* As

Psa. 118:22 (NIV) says, *"The stone the builders rejected has become the cornerstone."* Jesus quoted this verse in Matt. 21:42 (NIV) when He said to them, *"Have you never read in the Scriptures: 'The stone the builders rejected has become the cornerstone; the Lord has done this, and it is marvelous in our eyes?'"*

The tables are now turned, and the One men rejected and despised is now the One who is our Advocate, representing those of us who are His brethren and disciples before Father God, the impartial and holy Supreme Judge, in the Courts of Heaven. That is good news indeed for those who seek justice and who need relief and increased freedom and breakthrough from the ongoing accusations, influence, harassment and oppression from Satan and his demonic horde. I have good news for you: There is hope and help for you in the Courts of Heaven. You have come to the right place, because this book will show you how to get there, and what to do before you go there, after you arrive there, and after you return from there, in the Spirit.

I have provided a set of prayer templates in the chapters that follow, which the Holy Spirit has downloaded to me, and which have proved to be highly effective in helping the saints find new levels of freedom and breakthrough, and even upgraded identity in many cases. These prayers address and cover the 10 main areas of sin common to all bloodlines, and are designed to be comprehensive in scope and to leave no stone unturned, so it is a forensic-level approach, coupled with being led by Holy Spirit.

God perceives and understands sin differently than man does. This truth forces us to look inwardly at ourselves and let Him examine our hearts, if we truly desire to be pleasing to Him, and to walk in the light as He is in the light. David prayed in Psa. 139:23-24 (NIV), *"Search me, God, and know my heart; test me and know my anxious thoughts. See if there is any offensive way in me, and lead me in the way everlasting."* We need to do the same, on either a daily, weekly, monthly, or at least periodic basis.

In this regard, Rom. 14:23b (KJV) makes an interesting point. It says, *"Whatsoever is not of faith is sin."* That requires us to look at our motives, and how and why we do things, and not just what we do, since many things we do are from habit, custom and routine, and do not necessarily involve faith. Fortunately, the context of this Scripture is about comparing and contrasting faith with doubt and conviction, not habit and routine. Still, it is a sobering statement. 2 Cor. 5:7 (BSB, CSB, NKJV) says it best: *"For we walk by faith, not by sight."*

According to Heb. 11:6 (NIV), faith is required on our part to please God: *"And without faith it is impossible to please God, because anyone who comes to him must believe that he exists and that he rewards those who earnestly seek him."* Rom. 10:17 (BSB, NKJV) tells us that *"faith comes by hearing, and hearing by the word of God."* And, we know that faith was credited to Abraham as righteousness. Paul the Apostle said it well in Rom. 1:16-17 (NKJV): *"For I am not ashamed of the gospel of Christ, for it is the power of God to salvation for everyone who believes, for the Jew first and also for the Greek. For in it the righteousness of God is revealed from faith to faith; as it is written, 'The just shall live by faith.'"*

The Greek word used for "faith" is *pistis*, according to Strong's Greek 4102, and means faith or faithfulness. Faith in Scripture is synonymous with the words "overcome" or "victory" or "crown" (John 16:33; 1 Cor. 15:57; 2 Tim. 4:8; James 1:12; 1 Pet. 5:4; Rev. 12:11; Deut. 20:4; Prov. 21:31; Psa. 118:15).

1 John 5:4 (NIV) is an example of this:

> For everyone born of God overcomes the world. This is the victory that has overcome the world, even our faith.

According to Jas. 2:14-22 (NLT), faith without works is dead, and these two fit together hand in glove and cannot be separated.

> What good is it, dear brothers and sisters, if you say you have faith but don't show it by your actions? Can that kind of faith save anyone? Suppose you see a brother or sister who has no food or clothing, and you say, "Good-bye and have a good day; stay warm and eat well"—but then you don't give that person any food or clothing. What good does that do? So you see, faith by itself isn't enough. Unless it produces good deeds, it is dead and useless ...

> Don't you remember that our ancestor Abraham was shown to be right with God by his actions when he offered his son Isaac on the altar? You see, his faith and his actions worked together. His actions made his faith complete.

Faith is more than belief and mental assent. It involves action, is willing to take risks, and produces fruit. So, as I close this brief introduction, I invite you to exercise your faith and take a journey with me, one that will no doubt be a watershed event in your life. It is one that I have taken many times before, and I know from experience and can testify that what awaits you on the other side is more than you can ask, think or imagine, and that your life will never be the same again.

—BRUCE COOK, Ph.D., Th.D.
MAY 31, 2020 | PENTECOST

# FOREWORD

God is always speaking! John 1:1 (BSB, CSB, ESV, HCS, NASB, NIV, NKJV) says:

> *In the beginning was the Word, and the Word was with God, and the Word was God.*

Matt. 4:4 (NKJV) adds:

> *And, truly, "Man does not live by bread alone, but by every Word that proceeds from the mouth of God."*

I often imagine heaven like a huge radio station broadcasting a constant "rhema word," a NOW Word into the earth, 24 hours a day! Although God is always speaking, not everyone is hearing. Not everyone has cultivated a listening ear to hear what the Spirit is saying to the Church.

Over the last 20 years or so, God has been sending forth a clear and certain sound concerning Heaven's Courtroom. All over the world, people have been "tuning in" to this revelation.

In this book, we have an international, apostolic father who has succinctly and accurately captured this message. Then, with theological soundness and practical instruction, he has created the quintessential "textbook" on the topic. I believe this book will be referred to for decades to come as a definitive, working manual for those interested in operating in the Courts of Heaven.

Thorough, systematic, revelatory, practical and scriptural would all be words that I would use to describe this valuable book—a masterpiece!

## MY OWN HEAVENLY COURTROOM EXPERIENCE

It was about 30 years ago that God radically and completely changed my life in one experience. I had been in ministry by that time for about 15 years. We had had some moderate success, but always felt like something was lacking.

One day I was walking alone down the street, listening to my spiritual father talking on a cassette tape about forgiveness. For some reason that day, his words were setting my heart on fire! It was as though I was being arrested.

Then, without notice, I was suddenly caught up in an open vision. This is where the natural realm is suspended, and you are totally caught up in the spirit realm.

Before me, like a movie, was a heavenly Courtroom scene. God the Father was the righteous judge seated on a raised bench. To His right, down on the floor level, seated at a table, were a team of prosecuting attorneys. They had several long yellow legal pads filled with handwriting and accusations.

Also in the Courtroom was Jesus, the defense attorney, our Advocate with the Father. There were also numerous witnesses in the Courtroom who were observing the proceedings.

To my amazement, I saw myself seated in the witness stand just to the left of the judge. I looked beaten and battered, as the prosecuting attorneys, one at a time, would lash into me with various accusations. As I watched myself in the witness stand try to offer my defense, they would twist my words, manipulate the facts, and torment me unrelentingly. As one would become exhausted, he would sit down and another would take his place immediately, while continuing with the accusations. Truly, the Accuser goes night and day before the throne of God bringing accusations!

Looking at myself in the vision, I wondered when this demonic interrogation would end. I finally cried out in a loud voice in frustration in real life on the street, "Why is there no grace for me?"

Suddenly ... once again in real life, I heard the trumpet voice of God—like what John the Apostle heard on the Isle of Patmos—coming over my right shoulder and piercing my heart with the words, *"Judge not lest you be judged, for with the same measure you mete it out, it will be meted back to you again!"*

In a moment of blinding revelation, I now understood why there was so little grace for me. It was because I had offered so little grace to everyone else! I had been raised in a religious system that took pride in judging other churches, denominations, leaders, etc. I had freely judged many in the body of Christ throughout my entire life, and I was now reaping those same judgments against myself by the enemy.

I knew then intuitively what I had to do! While walking down the sidewalk, I began to release and to forgive everyone I could think of against whom I had held judgments, unforgiveness, or accusations of any kind. It probably took me about an hour to go through the list of all the people I had freely judged. One by one, I unlocked their prison doors and set them free.

Finally, when I had released everyone I could think of that I had judged, accused, or held unforgiveness toward, the open vision continued again right where it had left off. I was back in the heavenly Courtroom, except now, the whole atmosphere had changed! The prosecuting attorneys angrily began to throw all of their notebooks and legal materials into their briefcases, and to slam them shut, and then they stormed out of the Courtroom! I knew instantly by the Spirit they were now "unemployed"!

The Father looked at me from behind the bench and asked me, "Where are your accusers?" I said, "There are none, Lord." And then He nodded at me as if to say, "You are free to go!"

When I stepped down out of the witness stand, I felt as though 10,000 pounds of condemnation fell off of my shoulders, and I have walked free in that area ever since! Whom the Son sets free is free indeed!

I know that Heaven's Courtroom is real. I've been there! And, now I have the privilege to take other people there to be set free in their lives as well.

DENNIS WIEDRICK
Founder & President
Wiedrick & Associates, Apostolic Ministries
Calgary, AB Canada
Author: *A Royal Priesthood: Reigning with Christ through Intercession*

PART ONE

# PREPARING AND PRESENTING YOUR CASE IN THE COURTS OF HEAVEN

"LET US THEN APPROACH
GOD'S THRONE OF GRACE
WITH CONFIDENCE, SO THAT
WE MAY RECEIVE MERCY
AND FIND GRACE TO HELP
US IN OUR TIME OF NEED."

– HEBREWS 4:16 (NIV)

CHAPTER 1

# FAMILIES AND ANCESTRAL BLOODLINES

## THE DIFFERENCE BETWEEN GOD'S PLAN AND SATAN'S PLAN

God created humanity as male and female. All babies are born as either boys or girls. This same order, pattern and typology is reflected throughout the various species of animals and other life forms on earth, with only a few exceptions of microorganisms which are asexual. God designed families as the primary means, mode, method and mechanism by which reproduction, multiplication, discipleship, education, socialization, love, nurture, comfort, identity, affirmation, acceptance, honor, provision, protection, sonship, friendship, blessing, order, wealth transfer and generational inheritance, take place and occur in the earth. This is God's plan[1] and it is good,[2] as numerous Scriptures testify and confirm.

God thinks generationally, and is known and referred to in the Old Testament by the Jews as the God of Abraham, Isaac and Jacob. Prov. 13:22 (NIV) says, *"A good person leaves an inheritance for their children's children, but a sinner's wealth is stored up for the righteous."* Psa. 90:4 (ESV) records, *"For a thousand years in your sight are but as yesterday when it is past, or as a watch in the night."* 2 Pet. 3:8 (ESV) also notes, *"But do not overlook this one fact, beloved, that with the Lord one day is as a thousand years, and a thousand years as one day."* God is atemporal and exists outside of time. In fact, He created seasons and times.[3]

However, the enemy of our souls, Satan, also has a plan for families, and it is very different, and evil. His plan is to lie, deceive, divide, devour, disappoint, disillusion, depress, offend, wound, violate, traumatize, isolate, separate, sabotage, betray, abandon, reject, hate, accuse, abort, kill, steal and destroy, and to cause chaos, confusion, disorder and disunity.[4] So, families are the natural battleground and first line of defense in which these two opposing plans, cultures, kingdoms, and visions for the future are contested, presented, promoted, accepted or rejected, implemented, and manifested or expressed, in cities, communities, states, provinces, regions, nations and cultures.

Healthy families are intentional and purposeful about making such important choices. They teach ethical and/or godly values, create positive family traditions, promote interpersonal communication and group interaction, and set and enforce rules and boundaries. Unhealthy families, by contrast, often make such decisions with little forethought, or unknowingly, at a subconscious level, or spontaneously and irrationally at an emotional level, or even involuntarily when addiction is involved.

In addition to the soulish, carnal nature of mankind and the sin and temptation which so easily beset us, the sins of our forefathers, passed down through our respective ancestral bloodlines, are possibly the biggest single constraint we face in life on a personal basis. Let the weight of that sink in for a moment. A constraint is defined as a limitation or restriction. The focus of constraint theory to date has been on organizational, personal and environmental constraints,[5] and I believe it is possible that the sins of our forefathers, passed down through our respective ancestral bloodlines, are possibly the biggest single constraint we face personally. And, while we are not personally responsible for the sins of others, we nonetheless are influenced by and suffer from the effects and consequences of our forefathers' sins.[6]

Peter the Apostle refers to this unfortunate reality and state of affairs in his first epistle, *"For you know that it was not with perishable things such as silver or gold that **you were redeemed from the empty way of life handed down to you from your ancestors,** but with the precious blood of Christ, a lamb without blemish or defect"* (1 Pet. 1:18-19, NIV, author's emphasis). The Passion Translation is even more descriptive, stating, *"For you know that **your lives were ransomed once and for all from the empty and futile way of life handed down from generation to generation"*** (TPT, author's emphasis).

## SOURCE OF BLOODLINE CURSES

All of us have ancestors who were a complex mixture of good and evil, with some members of our bloodlines being more good than evil, while others were more evil than good. In fact, some ancestors may have been notoriously or infamously evil, while others may have been godly, acclaimed, revered, esteemed, and highly regarded saints. So, regardless of where we originated and descended from in natural terms, we have inherited from our biological, adoptive, blended, common law, foster, or step families or guardians, a mixture in terms of our bloodlines. This includes both hereditary and environmental factors, such as genes, genetics, norms, folkways, mores, beliefs, attitudes, values, prayers, mantles, blessings, heritage, reputation, curses, lies, sins, iniquities and transgressions.

Then, in addition, we have our extended families with cousins, uncles, aunts, grandparents, and great-grandparents, and those joined to our bloodlines through marriage or business covenants. Some of these relatives or those adjoined are people we have never even met and that we may know very little, if anything, about. Some of them may have been dead for many years before we were even born. However, such unconfessed and unrepented sins in our ancestral bloodlines, provide an outstanding claim, a legal right and an access point or open door, portal or gateway for Satan to accuse and attack us and our families.

# BREAKING THE POWER OF CURSES

Someone (hopefully you), sometime, somewhere, needs to stand in the gap and pray the prayers of repentance for your ancestral bloodline in order to break the generational cycles and patterns of curses, lies, transgressions, iniquities and sins that are common to most, if not all, bloodlines. Do you have the authority to do this? Yes, absolutely you do, if you have invited or accepted Jesus into your heart to be Lord and Savior of your life, and have confessed and repented of your personal sins, and have become a son or daughter of God, and are following Christ and His teachings as a disciple, and are being changed, transformed and sanctified by His word, His Spirit, and fellowship with and service to other saints.

Isaiah 59:16 (NKJV) says, *"He [God] saw that there was no man, And wondered that there was no intercessor; Therefore His own arm brought salvation for Him; And His own righteousness, it sustained Him."* Other translations render the phrase *"And wondered"* in this verse as *"He was amazed," "He was appalled,"* and *"He was astonished"* that there was no intercessor. This book is an invitation for you to fill that role in your family and your ancestral bloodline, as Daniel and Nehemiah and Ezra did, and to pray repentance for your bloodline through the prayer templates which are included in later chapters.

Satan is a deceiver, a legalist, and the accuser of the brethren (saints). The Greek word for "accuser" is *kategoros*, which means a plaintiff at law.[7] Elsewhere in Scripture, Satan is called our adversary. The Greek word for "adversary" is *antidikos*, which means "a prosecuting attorney arguing a case-at-law, an opponent at law, someone who brings formal charges."[8] Therefore, in order to beat Satan at his own game, it is much more strategic and effective to confront the archenemy of our souls in a courtroom in heaven first, before doing so on a battlefield on earth. This is divine order and wisdom. As we first deal with outstanding issues in our lives, our families, and our bloodlines through repentance in the Courts of Heaven, we will then see the results and fruit of that repentance begin to manifest on the earth.

WHAT WE ADDRESS IN THE COURTS OF HEAVEN BEGINS TO MANIFEST ON THE EARTH.

In the Courts of Heaven, we can face our Accuser(s) and hear and see the evidence and charges he has against us, and have Christ Jesus as our Advocate to defend us and refute this evidence, and to help us present our case, repent on behalf of our families and ancestral bloodlines, enter a plea, and obtain a verdict and legal judgment in our favor from the impartial, Supreme Judge, Father God, who rules justly in the Courts of Heaven.

Christ ransomed and redeemed us at the cross by paying the ultimate price, laying down His life for the sins of the world, and shedding His blood as an atoning sacrifice and propitiation "outside the camp" or outside the city gates as a sinless lamb without blemish or spot. But, even though the work of Jesus the Messiah at Calvary was a finished, "once and for all" work, as saints today, we must still claim, receive and appropriate the benefits His sacrifice provided and made possible for us, and enforce the great victory Christ won when He defeated death, plundered hell, and brought back the keys of death, hell and hades. Rev. 12:11 (NKJV) says, *"And they overcame him by the blood of the Lamb and by the word of their testimony, and they did not love their lives to the death."*

Furthermore, even though Christ's sacrifice on the cross is a finished work, Satan's work is not finished. 1 Pet. 5:8 (NKJV) says, *"Be sober, be vigilant; because your adversary the devil walks about like a roaring lion, seeking whom he may devour."* The NIV says, *"Be alert and of sober mind. Your enemy the devil prowls around like a roaring lion looking for someone to devour."* It is worth noting that The Passion Translation (TPT) includes the word "incessantly" in this verse (author's emphasis): *"Be well balanced and always alert, because your enemy, the devil, roams around **incessantly**, like a roaring lion looking for its prey to devour."*

The word "incessantly" suggests that Satan, although a defeated foe, is continuously or in a nonstop manner, trying to accuse, attack and deceive God's people in an effort to populate hell, expand his own kingdom of darkness, and fulfill his mission and purpose to kill, steal and destroy. Rev. 12:10 (NKJV, author's emphasis) confirms this: *Then I heard a loud voice saying in heaven, "Now salvation, and strength, and the kingdom of our God, and the power of his Christ have come, **for the accuser of our brethren, who accused them before our God day and night,** has been cast down."*

So, it makes great sense for us to want to move beyond living in a defensive posture only from Eph. 6:10-17 and experiencing repeated spiritual warfare over the same issues or territory, and to engage Eph. 2:5-6 and 2 Cor. 10:3-5 in the Courts of Heaven to address the spiritual roots in our ancestral bloodlines, that are behind this ongoing warfare.[9] When we do this, we will obtain a greater measure of freedom, breakthrough and relief that will in turn help us to produce more fruit and an abundant harvest during our time on earth. That is what this book is designed and intended to help you and your family experience. But, this strategy and course of action is a conscious, deliberate choice, and requires courage and action on your part, so choose wisely.

Jesus has other work that He is busily engaged in in heaven, where He is seated at the right hand of God, since He successfully completed His previous mission and assignment on earth. Today, He serves as our High Priest, Mediator, and Advocate, among other ongoing responsibilities. Jesus is also our Heavenly Intercessor (Heb. 7:25) and is preparing a place for us to dwell eternally with Him (John 14:1-3). In the future, as both the seed of David and the Son of God, He will open the scroll and its seven seals in heaven at the appointed time, and return to earth as King of kings and Lord of lords, where He will reign for a thousand years.[10]

The following Scriptures highlight these important roles that Jesus is, and has been, fulfilling in heaven ever since His ascension, each of which benefits us as saints in significant ways. These crucial roles are addressed below in the order of High Priest, Mediator, and Advocate.

# JESUS, OUR HIGH PRIEST

Heb. 4:14-16 (NIV, author's emphasis) says:

> Therefore, **since we have a great high priest who has ascended into heaven, Jesus the Son of God, let us hold firmly to the faith we profess. For we do not have a high priest who is unable to empathize with our weaknesses, but we have one who has been tempted in every way, just as we are—yet he did not sin.** Let us then approach God's throne of grace with confidence, so that we may receive mercy and find grace to help us in our time of need.

This confidence must not be in the flesh, but in Christ alone. And this confidence, when mixed with faith, a knowledge of God's nature and character, and a personal relationship with God, results in a healthy, realistic expectation toward God. Heb. 11:6 (NKJV) states, "*But without faith it is impossible to please Him, for he who comes to God must believe that He is, and that He is a rewarder of those who diligently seek Him.*" Because of Christ, who showed us the Father, and is seated at His right hand, we can find courage and confidence to come before Him in the Courts of Heaven to plead our case and face our Accuser(s).

Much additional information and detail about Christ's role as our eternal High Priest, are found in Heb. 8:1-10:24. There, the priesthood of Christ in heaven, functioning in the lineage and order of Melchizedek, is compared and contrasted to the earthly priesthood of those functioning in the lineage and order of Aaron and Levi. The conclusion is that Christ's priesthood is superior in every way.

# JESUS, OUR MEDIATOR

And, in case you are wondering what this heavenly venue looks like, Heb. 12:22-24 (NLT, author's emphasis) describes it:

> No, you have come to Mount Zion,[11] to the city of the living God, the heavenly Jerusalem, and to countless thousands of angels in a joyful gathering. You have come to the assembly of God's firstborn children, whose names are written in heaven. **You have come to God himself, who is the judge over all things.** You have come to the spirits of the righteous ones in heaven who have now been made perfect. **You have come to Jesus, the one who mediates the new covenant between God and people,** and to the sprinkled blood, which speaks of forgiveness instead of crying out for vengeance like the blood of Abel.

The blood of Jesus speaks on our behalf in heaven from the mercy seat.

# JESUS, OUR ADVOCATE

According to Merriam-Webster.com, the word advocate, in a legal sense, is defined as "one who pleads the cause of another, specifically : one who pleads the cause of another before a tribunal or judicial court."[12] Jesus is our legal representative, and 1 John 1:5-2:2 (NKJV, author's emphasis) notes:

> This is the message which we have heard from Him and declare to you, that God is light and in Him is no darkness at all. If we say that we have fellowship with Him, and walk in darkness, we lie and do not practice the truth. But if we walk in the light as He is in the light, we have fellowship with one another, and **the blood of Jesus Christ His Son cleanses us from all sin.**
>
> If we say that we have no sin, we deceive ourselves, and the truth is not in us. If we confess our sins, He is faithful and just to forgive us our sins and to cleanse us from all unrighteousness. If we say that we have not sinned, we make Him a liar, and His word is not in us. My little children, these things I write to you, so that you may not sin. **And if anyone sins, we have an Advocate with the Father, Jesus Christ the righteous.** And He Himself is the propitiation for our sins, and not for ours only but also for the whole world.

As our Advocate, Jesus serves as our legal counsel and defense attorney in the Courts of Heaven and represents us against Satan's accusations and charges. Accordingly, I refer to the saints who make appearances in this heavenly court system as a Defendant, individually, and as Defendants, collectively, when more than one person is presenting a case.[13] Jesus' track record is perfect and He has never lost a case. So, as good as Perry Mason, Ben Matlock, Barnaby Jones, Oliver Wendell Holmes Sr. and Jr., Learned Hand, William Blackstone, and other barristers, attorneys, lawyers, judges and law firms on earth—both real and fictional—may be, you are in the best hands possible.

# PLEADING YOUR CASE

You and Jesus are enough to prevail; however, you may enjoy your experience more and get more out of it if you know or can find and recruit one or more seasoned, prophetic seers to join your legal team in the Courts of Heaven as your case is being presented, and help address the evidence that is against you in your ancestral bloodline. But, if not, you can initiate and participate in one or more sessions on your own. Just be aware that it will potentially be more challenging and difficult for you to imagine or visualize what is happening during your time in heaven, if you are not a seer yourself.

In that case, you would have to depend almost entirely on the Holy Spirit to help guide you, and utilize your spiritual hearing and also your other senses in whatever way the Holy Spirit works with you and communicates to you. Some people have a "gut feeling" or an "inner knowing," for example, and often can feel a release in their spirit when an area of sin has been prayed through and repented of. And, of course, you will have access to the protocol, process and prayers in this book to help you navigate the Courts of Heaven.

One of the reasons I wrote this book is that currently I am not aware of any standard or protocol which exists or has gained widespread acceptance, as to what constitutes and needs to be included in a Courts of Heaven session, or how many sessions are needed or optimal to address an issue or present a case or obtain a verdict. Nor is there any standard or protocol I am aware of for the most effective approach and order or sequence of events to follow while in the Courts of Heaven. Nor, how does one measure or assess the results or outcome of a session, and determine whether or not it has been effective or productive?

These and other such "how to" questions remain largely unaddressed to the best of my knowledge, despite an increasing number of books written on this subject—most notably by Robert Henderson, who helped pioneer this field and started teaching on it around 2010 and wrote the first book on it in 2014, plus a few others who have benefited from his influence.[14] Therefore, these questions invite and deserve a response. This book has been written in an effort to answer these and other questions and to provide a practical, "how to" process and protocol using best practices for accessing and navigating the Courts of Heaven, on either a one-time or ongoing basis.

## WHAT IS THE COURTS OF HEAVEN?

It is also debatable whether a working definition currently exists for the commonly-used phrase, "the Courts of Heaven," other than as an unspecified location in the Third Heaven, and a place to seek justice from God and relief and freedom from Satanic and demonic influence. In order to bring clarity and agreement on terms, I therefore propose the following as a definition:

## THE COURTS OF HEAVEN: A DEFINITION

The Courts of Heaven is a fully-developed, fully-functioning court system in heaven where the children of God (saints) are represented by a heavenly Advocate (Jesus) and can present their case, face their Accuser(s), hear the charges against them, offer repentance, enter a plea, and receive a verdict from God the Supreme Judge, and can find increased relief, freedom, and breakthrough from Satanic and demonic accusation, attack, harrassment, hindrance, influence, interference, intimidation, opposition, oppression, resistance, schemes, strategies, and/or torment.

# COURTROOM PROCESS

It is my opinion that there is more than one way to operate and function in the Courts of Heaven, and that numerous people have tried different approaches in recent years for different reasons and with different motives and goals and understandings, with varying degrees of success. They have had a wide range of outcomes and results, including many outstanding and dramatic successes, but also some dismal failures, mainly due to a lack of knowledge and understanding, and perhaps some wrong or false expectations about the Courts of Heaven. I am hopeful that this book will help to reduce, mitigate or eliminate the failures, and increase the successes, by applying what is taught and shared here.

Moreover, this evolving area of ministry and study to date has an abundant and vigorous theology and numerous testimonies from satisfied participants, but very little empirical data. So, in my opinion, it is not a question of there being only one right way or approach, but of observing, obeying and honoring heaven's protocol and sharing best practices to achieve optimal, maximum effectiveness, efficiency, and results. It is also about recognizing and agreeing on the need to establish some baseline definitions and terminology for the Courts of Heaven, some of which I have provided here.

Furthermore, we should aim for an approach that allows for flexibility rather than rigidity for our time in the Courts of Heaven, to allow for and follow the leading, guiding and prompting of the Holy Spirit. But, this requires that those participating be filled with the Spirit and be sensitive, surrendered, and submitted to the Spirit in order to have a positive and productive experience and outcome while in the Courts of Heaven. Invite and allow the Holy Spirit to participate with you, and give Holy Spirit permission to interrupt you and surprise you during your session(s) as He leads and guides. Holy Spirit knows best.

Some people take this approach to an extreme and have no protocol or process for their session(s), except for being Spirit-led and relying on their own spiritual hearing or seer gift, or other seers who are part of their session. That approach may be fine for single issues but may not produce the best outcomes for cleansing ancestral bloodlines. It also limits access to the Courts of Heaven to only those who are seers and/or those who know or can access seers. This kind of free flow, unstructured approach may often result in a shorter, noncomprehensive session.

Others take a different, more structured approach and may have written prayers, protocol and process in place to use for their time in the Courts of Heaven. These tools can be very useful in helping you to facilitate an orderly flow and heartfelt repentance, and to cover a large number of possible areas of sin in your ancestral bloodline as quickly and efficiently as possible. This approach can also be taken to an extreme and can easily dominate or overpower a session, and leave little room or time for hearing from or being led by the Spirit, if you are not careful. So, I believe it is important to find a balance between the two, and that is one reason I have written this book in order to help open up access to the Courts of Heaven to the entire body of Christ, by providing a protocol, process and set of prayer templates to help guide you.

Some people want to address one issue at a time, and like to have multiple sessions in the Courts of Heaven over a longer period of time that are all focused around one or possibly two issues at most, and are shorter in duration. Others prefer to eat the whole elephant at once, so to speak, and to deal with all of their ancestral bloodline issues at once as part of a longer session. One way is not better than the other; it is more a matter of your personal preference, time availability, general health and wellbeing of the Defendant(s), your own sense of urgency and priority in addressing these issues, your goal for the session, the cost involved (if any), and the experience level, gifting and maturity of the prophetic seers you are working with, if any.

So, my recommendation, based on extensive personal experience[15] with several thousand different individuals and many hundreds of families[16] in the Courts of Heaven, is to integrate these two approaches described above and incorporate elements from both, so that you can include the best of both in your session. As a rule of thumb, the longer the session, the more structure you will need. And, although this book focuses primarily on Courtroom process, protocol and prayers of repentance to help you cleanse your ancestral bloodline, those of you who are issue-focused and interested in resolving a single issue rather than bloodline-focused, will also benefit from reading and applying this book. The two go together and, in my opinion, it is not really feasible to separate current issues from your ancestral bloodline.

I have heard of sessions in the Courts of Heaven that were five minutes in length, and I have been part of sessions that were five hours in length. Some people have had one longer session, and others have had two or three sessions, up to as many as 10 or 15 shorter sessions. Certainly, the amount of time spent in the Courts of Heaven is not the key driver or gating factor for getting results, and it is much more about the quality of time we spend there, rather than the quantity. But, it is hard to imagine that much of significance can be accomplished or occur in less than 30 minutes at a minimum, and typically several hours are required for each session on average.

The Holy Spirit plays an integral part in what happens in the Courts of Heaven, just as Jesus and Father God do. John 14:26 (NKJV) says, "But the Helper, the Holy Spirit, whom the Father will send in my name, He will teach you all things, and bring to your remembrance all things that I said to you." John 16:13a (NASB, NIV) adds, "But when He, the Spirit of truth, comes, He will guide you into all the truth." So, while it is helpful to follow a proven and tested process and protocol, we also are taught and guided by the Holy Spirit in the Courts of Heaven, and we need to adjust accordingly and spontaneously in real time as led, prompted, nudged or directed by the Spirit.

Some of the factors to consider when planning a Courts of Heaven session include, but are not limited to, the following:

1. the motivation, expectations and goals for the session;

2. whether a laser-focused, single-issue-based approach is desired, or whether a more comprehensive, in-depth session is targeted for ancestral bloodline cleansing;

3. the overall health and wellness of the Defendant(s);

4. how much time and energy and resources are available for the session;

5. the nature, number and severity of issues that will be addressed in the session;

6. how much, if any, spiritual preparation has been done by the Defendant(s) in advance of the session, including prayer, fasting, reflection, repentance, forgiveness, reading books, and/or watching videos;

7. if more than one Defendant is participating in this session, how many Defendants will be part of the session, and what type of relationship do they have with each other;

8. which Court(s) will have jurisdiction for this case;

9. whether or not any seers will be part of the session; and

10. if yes to #9, how much experience, training and knowledge these seers have regarding the Courts of Heaven; what level of spiritual gifting, character and maturity they have; and whether or not they have been commissioned or ordained in ministry, and for how long.

So, hopefully this discussion has given you some things to think and pray about, and consider further, and has encouraged you with renewed hope and fresh ideas to pray for your family and to repent for your ancestral bloodline in the manner outlined in this book. These prayers can potentially change your future, and that of your family, and I have seen and witnessed many examples of that over the years, and experienced it myself. We will dive deeper into the details of that in subsequent chapters.

# AN INVITATION

As this introductory chapter comes to a close, I invite you to choose God's plan for your family, and for your own life, and to reject Satan's plan. I also invite you to continue reading and to go with me on a mission and adventure of great importance and consequence in the pages that follow, as you learn how to effectively navigate the Courts of Heaven, face your Accuser(s), enter your plea, repent for the sins in your ancestral bloodline, present your case, secure a favorable verdict from the impartial and Supreme Judge, gain increased freedom, become more fruitful, enlarge your harvest, stand in the gap for your family, and be able to enforce and maintain your new level of increased freedom in an ongoing manner. We turn our attention now to Chapter 2.

## ENDNOTES

1. See for example Gen. 1:26-28, 2:15-25; Deut. 6:6-9, 11:18-20; Psa. 1:1-6, 68:5-6; Prov. 7:1-3, 13:22, 22:6, 31:1-31; Eccl. 2:26; Isa. 57:8; Matt. 19:4-6; 1 Cor. 6:12-7:17; Eph. 5:22-6:4; Jas. 1:27; 1 Tim. 5:3-16; Tit. 2:2-6.

2. See for example Gen. 1:31; Exo. 33:19; 1 Chron. 16:34; Psa. 25:7-8, 31:19-20, 34:8, 84:11, 86:5, 100:5, 106:1, 119:68, 145:9; Nah. 1:7; Matt. 7:11, 19:17; Mark 10:18; Luke 18:19; Rom. 11:22; Jas. 1:17; 1 Tim. 4:4.

3. See for example Gen. 1:1-2:25; Job 38:1-41:34; Eccl. 3:1-17; Josh. 10:1-15; Isa. 38:1-8; Acts 17:22-31; 1 Thess. 5:1-11.

4.  See for example Gen. 3:1-24; Exo. 20:14; Prov. 6:32-35; Job 1:6-12, 2:1-7; Isa. 14:12-15; Ezek. 28:11-19; Zech. 3:1-2; Matt. 5:27-28; Luke 4:1-13, 22:3-23; John 8:44, 10:10, 13:27; 1 Cor. 6:9-10; 1 Thess. 4:3-7; Heb. 13:4; Jas. 3:14-16, 4:1-4, 7; 1 Pet. 5:8; Rev. 12:1-17, 21:8, 22:12-16.

5.  The Theory of Constraints was developed and communicated by manufacturing expert Eliyahu M. Goldratt and Jeff Cox in 1984 through their novel, *The Goal: A Process of Ongoing Improvement*, Great Barrington, MA: North River Press. They define a Constraint as anything that limits a system from achieving a higher performance versus its goal. For further reference, see also a discussion of constraints by Will Meier, 2019, *Leaders for Life: Creating Champions Through the NOW Leadership Process*, Lakebay, WA: Kingdom House Publishing, pp. 126-28.

6.  See for example Deut. 5:9; Exo. 34:7; Num. 14:18; Psa. 79:8, 109:14; Isa. 65:6-7; Jer. 32:18; Ezek. 18:1-32; Matt. 12:36; Rom. 14:12; 2 Cor. 5:10; 1 Pet. 1:17-20.

7.  Strong's Greek, 2725. See for example John 8:10; Acts 23:30, 35, 24:8, 25:16, 18; and especially Rev. 12:10. For a fuller context, read Rev. 12:9-11.

8.  Strong's Greek, 476. See for example Luke 18:3 and 1 Pet. 5:8 (NKJV).

9.  I have reserved a fuller discussion of Eph. 2:5-6 and its significance for the Courts of Heaven, for Chapter 2. In regards to 2 Cor. 10:3-5, it is my opinion that some of the weapons we (saints or Christians) fight with that have divine power to demolish strongholds, include not only those we use on earth, but also in the Courts of Heaven, such as prayer, intercession, repentance, forgiveness, humility, praise, honor, mercy, the gift of tongues, and other similar attitudes, virtues, graces, gifts, and/or actions. Also, we do not wage war in the flesh or as the world does, because those without Christ have not been regenerated or redeemed or born again, and do not have the mind of Christ or the blood of Christ or the Holy Spirit or the gifts of the Spirit, and so they do not have access to the Courts of Heaven, as I explain more fully in Chapter 2.

10. See for example Psa. 89:35-36; 132:11; Isa. 9:6-7; Jer. 23:5; Matt. 1:1-17, 22:42; Luke 2:1-3:38; John 7:42; Rom. 1:1-4; 1 Cor. 15:12-58; Gal. 4:4-5; 1 Thess. 4:13-18; 2 Tim. 2:8-12; Rev. 5:1-11:19, 12:1-22:21, 20:4-6.

11. Mount Zion here refers to the Mountain of the House of the Lord, which is referred to in Isa. 2:1 5 and Micah 4:1-5. See Dr. Bruce Cook, *The 8th Mountain: How the Mountain of the Lord Transforms and Empowers Leaders to Influence the 7 Mountains of Culture*, 2017, Lakebay, WA: Kingdom House Publishing. See also Don Nori Sr. and Amb. Clyde Rivers, *The Forgotten Mountain: Your Place of Peace in a World at War*, 2016, Shippensburg, PA: Destiny Image Publishers, Inc.

12. https://www.merriam-webster.com/dictionary/advocate.

13. Dr. Francis Myles has called the saints Plaintiffs in his book *Issuing Divine Restraining Orders from the Courts of Heaven*. From my perspective, as long

as the saints pray the repentance prayers in this book, the practical effect and outcome will be the same from either legal position: The saints will win their Court case and they will gain an increased—often massive— new level of spiritual freedom.

14. A few of Robert Henderson's many book titles on this subject include *Operating in the Courts of Heaven*, *Unlocking Destiny in the Courts of Heaven*, *Releasing Healing in the Courts of Heaven*, *Prayers & Declarations that Open the Courts of Heaven*, *Petitioning the Courts of Heaven During Times of Crisis*, *The Cloud of Witnesses in the Courts of Heaven*, *Unlocking Wealth from the Courts of Heaven*, *Receiving Generational Blessings from the Courts of Heaven*, and *Father, Friend, and Judge: Three Dimensions of Prayer that Receive Answers from Heaven*. The first full-length book on this topic was written in 2014 by Robert Henderson. A sampling of other authors includes: Dr. Francis Myles, *Issuing Divine Restraining Orders from the Courts of Heaven*, *Idols Riot! Prosecuting Idols and Evil Altars in the Courts of Heaven* (with Katie Souza); *Dangerous Prayers from the Courts of Heaven that Destroy Evil Altars*; Beverley Watkins, *The Trading Floors of Heaven*; Natasha Grbich, *Repentance: Cleansing Your Generational Bloodline*; Brigette Marx, *The Seven Heavenly Courts*; Praying Medic, *Defeating Your Adversary in the Court of Heaven*, and *Operating in the Court of Angels*; and Dr. Ron Horner, *The Courts of Heaven: An Introduction*, *Engaging the Courts for Your City*, *Engaging the Courts of Heaven for Ownership & Order*, *Engaging the Help Desk of the Courts of Heaven*, *Engaging the Courts of Healing & the Healing Garden*, *Releasing Bonds from the Courts of Heaven*, *Overcoming Verdicts from the Courts of Hell: Releasing False Judgments*, *Engaging the Mercy Court of Heaven*, *Four Keys to Defeating Accusations*, *Overcoming the False Verdicts of Freemasonry*, and *Engaging the Courts of Heaven: Maximizing the Power of the Courts of Heaven*.

15. This is based on my experience with Robert Henderson and his ministries GPEC and Global Reformers, where I serve as a Hub Leader and Territorial Director for the Pacific Northwest region. I have facilitated and led well over 2,500 sessions as a Courtroom Navigator and Magistrate in the Courts of Heaven for a large number of individuals and families in over 25-30 nations. To learn more about Robert Henderson and his ministries GPEC and Global Reformers, please visit the following websites: https://gpec.world; https://globalreformers.com; and https://roberthendersonministries.org and follow them on social media.

16. In addition to scheduling sessions in the Courts of Heaven for individuals, couples and families, my team and I also facilitate sessions for businesses, nonprofit organizations, cities, states and nations. To learn more about my ministry and how my team and I can help you, please visit my website https://thecourtsofheaven.org. To schedule a session, click on the Sign Up page https://thecourtsofheaven.org/register/. Fill in the requested information and click "Submit."

## CHAPTER 2
# PREPARING TO ENTER THE COURTS OF HEAVEN

As you prepare to enter the Courts of Heaven and present your case, there are at least several things you may want to consider, be aware of, and take care of well in advance of entering the Courtroom. Some of these are logistical and some are spiritual. We will also discuss legal standing and governing law in this chapter.

Among logistical considerations are to find a comfortable place for your session, make sure you are in a private and quiet location, that you are rested, that you are dressed comfortably, that you have a box of facial tissues nearby, that you have a bottle or two of cold water on hand or your favorite beverage, that you have decided whether or not to invite seers for your session, that you have sufficient resources if there is a session fee or donation required by the seers, and that you try to record the session if possible so that you can access the recording later if you so desire. For those who will be doing their session online, then you will need to have a camera-enabled smart device such as a laptop or desktop computer, tablet or smart phone available, and access to a high speed Internet connection (wifi).

Among spiritual considerations to prepare for your session, please try to read at least a few of Robert Henderson's many books on the Courts of Heaven, and/or view some of his video teachings which are posted online. It would also be helpful for you to spend some time praying and repenting of any known personal sins, forgiving others who have sinned against you, and possibly fasting in advance if so led. Also, if you do not hear from the Holy Spirit on a regular basis, and/or have not used your sanctified imagination before, or very often, you may want to pray and ask God to help you increase your gifts of seeing and hearing in the Spirit. You might also seek prayer for that from one or more ministry leaders you trust.

God sees and understands the purpose and function of law differently than man does, and places it in the context of covenant, not just community or society. Heb. 10:16 (NKJV) says, *"This is the covenant that I will make with them after those days, says the Lord: I will put my laws into their hearts, and in their minds I will write them."* We are beneficiaries and partakers of the new covenant that Jesus instituted by His sacrificial death on the cross and the shedding of His precious blood, according to Heb. 8:6-9:28. God wants us, as His sons and daughters, to internalize His laws in our hearts and do good to others as we have opportunity, not just live by an external code or set of rules.[1] That is the bigger picture.

Jesus once told the Pharisees in Mark 2:27-28 (NIV):

*"The Sabbath was made for man, not man for the Sabbath. So the Son of Man is Lord even of the Sabbath."*

Jesus then asked the religious leaders in a Jewish synagogue this question in Mark 3:4-5 (NIV, author's emphasis):

*"**Which is lawful on the Sabbath: to do good, or to do evil, to save life or to kill?**" But they remained silent. He [Jesus] looked around at them in anger and, deeply distressed at their stubborn hearts, said to the man, "Stretch out your hand." He stretched it out, and his hand was completely restored.*

Thus, I believe it is necessary that you have a saving relationship with Jesus in order to access the Courts of Heaven. Otherwise, Jesus would not be your Advocate to defend you and the blood of Jesus would not be speaking on your behalf, your sins would not be forgiven, you would not be born again and adopted into the family of God, and the Holy Spirit would not be living inside of you to help guide you, comfort you, teach you, and lead you into all truth. For unbelievers, their sins would still be separating them from God. This right to appear in the Courts of Heaven is called **standing**, which is a legal term, and all saints have this right because of the blood of Jesus, His righteousness and finished work on the cross, His ongoing work in heaven, and our relationship to Him as a new creation and as joint heirs.

In regard to standing, Paul the Apostle wrote in 1 Tim. 1:9 (AMP, author's emphasis):

*[U]nderstanding the fact that **law is not enacted for the righteous person [the one in right standing with God]**, but for lawless and rebellious people, for the ungodly*

and sinful, for the irreverent and profane, for those who kill their fathers or mothers, for murderers.

Rom. 8:30 adds (NLT, author's emphasis):

And having chosen them, he called them to come to him. **And having called them, he gave them right standing with himself. And having given them right standing, he gave them his glory.**

So, it is clear that the saints—those who are converts and disciples of Christ—are in right standing with God as a gift of grace. Rom. 3:22-24 (NLT, author's emphasis) says:

**We are made right with God by placing our faith in Jesus Christ.** And this is true for everyone who believes, no matter who we are. For everyone has sinned; we all fall short of God's glorious standard. **Yet God, with undeserved kindness, declares that we are righteous.** He did this through Christ Jesus when he freed us from the penalty for our sins.

Rom. 5:17 (NLT, author's emphasis) adds:

For the sin of this one man, Adam, caused death to rule over many. But even greater is **God's wonderful grace and his gift of righteousness,** for all who receive it will live in triumph over sin and death through this one man, Jesus Christ.

Again, God's gift of His righteousness to us through Christ is a gift of grace.

1 Cor. 1:30 (NLT, author's emphasis) says:

> *God has united you with Christ Jesus. For our benefit God made him to be wisdom itself. **Christ made us right with God;** he made us pure and holy, and he freed us from sin.*

2 Cor. 5:19-21 (NLT, author's emphasis) adds:

> *For God was in Christ, reconciling the world to himself, no longer counting people's sins against them. And he gave us this wonderful message of reconciliation. So we are Christ's ambassadors; God is making his appeal through us. We speak for Christ when we plead, "Come back to God!" **For God made Christ, who never sinned, to be the offering for our sin, so that we could be made right with God through Christ. Our right standing with God is purely and solely made possible through our faith in and saving relationship to, Christ, as a gift from God.***

Finally, Gal. 2:16 (NLT, author's emphasis) states:

> *Yet we know that **a person is made right with God by faith in Jesus Christ,** not by obeying the [Mosaic] law. And we have believed in Christ Jesus, so that **we might be made right with God because of our faith in Christ,** not because we have obeyed the law. For no one will ever be made right with God by obeying the law.*

The Scriptures are abundantly clear and in agreement on this foundational point that as children of God, we have right standing with Him through our faith in and saving relationship to

Christ, as a gift of grace from God. This legal standing with God is what gives us access to the Courts of Heaven.

# LEGAL STANDING

According to Wikipedia, "In law, standing or *locus standi* is the term for the ability of a party to demonstrate to the court sufficient connection to and harm from the law or action challenged to support that party's participation in the case. Standing exists from one of three causes:

- The party is directly subject to an adverse effect by the statute or action in question, and the harm suffered will continue unless the court grants relief in the form of damages or a finding that the law either does not apply to the party or that the law is void or can be nullified. This is called the "something to lose" doctrine, in which the party has standing because they will be directly harmed by the conditions for which they are asking the court for relief.

- The party is not directly harmed by the conditions by which they are petitioning the court for relief but asks for it because the harm involved has some reasonable relation to their situation, and the continued existence of the harm may affect others who might not be able to ask a court for relief. In the United States, this is the grounds for asking for a law to be struck down as violating the First Amendment to the Constitution of the United States, because while the plaintiff might not be directly affected, the law might so adversely affect others that one might never know what was not done or created by those who fear they would become subject to the law—the so-called "chilling effects" doctrine.

- The party is granted automatic standing by act of law. Under some environmental laws in the United States, a party may sue someone causing pollution to certain waterways without a federal permit, even if the party suing is not harmed by the pollution being generated. The law allows them to receive attorney's fees if they substantially prevail in the action. In some U.S. states, a person who believes a book, film or other work of art is obscene may sue in their own name to have the work banned directly without having to ask a District Attorney to do so."[2]

It is easy to see, using a spiritual lens or paradigm, that the saints of God have legal standing under the first cause listed above, since the harm suffered from Satan's accusations and attacks will continue, unless addressed and dealt with in the Courts of Heaven, and the saints of the Most High have something to lose if these accusations and attacks continue unabated and are not stopped or halted.

The second cause listed above also is fertile ground for the children of God from which to seek relief in the Courts of Heaven, since many of us have family members who are being and/or have been accused and attacked by Satan and his demonic horde. This could include spouses, children, grandchildren, parents, siblings, uncles, aunts, cousins, etc. We have standing to pray for them in the Courts of Heaven.

The third cause above is also applicable to the saints of God, because we have an act of law which grants us automatic standing in the Courts of Heaven to seek relief for others from the effects of such things as pandemics, natural disasters, terrorist attacks, and other damaging or deadly plans, plots, schemes, stratagems, technologies and/or weapons of the enemy. Luke 10:19 (NASB) says, "Behold, I have given you authority to tread on serpents and scorpions, and over all the power of the enemy, and nothing will injure you." James 5:16b (NIV) adds, "The prayer of a righteous person is powerful and effective."

# GOVERNING LAW

Praying for others is also a commandment rather than an option. 1 Tim. 2:1-6 (NIV) says:

> I urge, then, first of all, that petitions, prayers, intercession and thanksgiving be made for all people — for kings and all those in authority, that we may live peaceful and quiet lives in all godliness and holiness. This is good, and pleases God our Savior, who wants all people to be saved and to come to a knowledge of the truth. For there is one God and one mediator between God and mankind, the man Christ Jesus, who gave himself as a ransom for all people. This has now been witnessed to at the proper time.

So, the sons and daughters of God (saints) qualify for standing on all three of the legally-defined and -accepted causes of standing, in a spiritual sense, under the laws of God. We have every right to present our own cases and to bring cases affecting others in the Courts of Heaven. The law of God is higher and greater than both common law and civil law—the two dominant, prevalent legal systems in the earth which are used to help govern nations.

Common law is defined as "the body of law developed in England primarily and derived from judicial decisions based on custom and precedent, rather than statutes or codes, and constituting the basis of the English legal system."[3] It is used in the United Kingdom, the U.S. (except for Louisiana), Canada, Australia, New Zealand, Bahamas, Barbados, Bermuda, Bhutan, British Virgin Islands, Cayman Islands, Cyprus, Fiji, Gibraltar, Grenada, most of India, Hong Kong, Singapore, and other nations.[4]

The main areas and/or branches of common law include, but are not limited to, administrative law, admiralty or maritime law, business law, civil law, criminal law, constitutional law, contract law, employment law, environmental law, family law, real estate law, military law, tax law, bankruptcy law, wills and trusts law, estate law, probate law, intellectual property law, international law, securities law, personal injury law, etc.

Civil law has at least two definitions: 1) "the part of the legal system that deals with people's relationships, property, and business agreements, rather than with criminal activity," and 2) "a legal system based on ancient Roman law, which is used in many countries. In this system a court makes decisions based on a set of recorded laws rather than on the decision of a judge or jury."[5]

A sampling of nations governed by civil law includes France, Germany, Greece, Italy, Japan, Mexico, Romania, Russia, Spain, Thailand, Austria, Albania, Armenia, Angola, Andora, Aruba, Argentina, Azerbaijan, Belarus, Belgium, Brazil, Benin, Bulgaria, Burundi, China, Cambodia, Chad, Chile, Colombia, Costa Rica,

Croatia, Czech Republic, Curacao, Denmark, Dominican Republic, Ecuador, El Salvador, Estonia, Finland, Iceland, Norway, South Korea, Sweden, and Switzerland.[6]

The main difference between these two systems is that in common law nations, case law—consisting of published judicial opinions—is of primary importance, whereas in civil law systems, codified statutes predominate. These statutes typically originate from parliaments and/or legislatures, but historically, they have also derived from other authoritative sources such as emperors, czars, kings and rulers (the Code of Hammurabi and the Justinian Code, for example). In actual practice, many countries use a mix of features from both systems of law. Some nations also use a hybrid of civil law and religious law to govern, typically either canon law (Christian), Jewish law (Halakha) or Islamic law (Sharia).[7]

**LAW CANNOT PRODUCE OR MANDATE LOVE.** God's law, by contrast, is from above, from God the Sovereign Creator and Sustainer of Life, El Shaddai, Elohim, Jehovah, Yahweh. The Great Commandment is called the "royal law" in Jas. 2:8 because this involves love, something that law cannot produce or mandate apart from God. Matt. 22:37-40 (NASB) says:

*And He [Jesus] said to him, "You shall love the Lord your God with all your heart, and with all your soul, and with all your mind." This is the great and foremost commandment. The second is like it, "You shall love your neighbor as yourself." On these two commandments depend the whole Law and the Prophets.*

The fact that God's law is above man's law is referenced other places, too, including Isa. 55:8-9 (NKJV):

> "For my thoughts are not your thoughts, nor are your ways my ways," says the Lord. "For as the heavens are higher than the earth, so are my ways higher than your ways, and my thoughts than your thoughts."

Gal. 5:22-23 (NIV) says:

> But the fruit of the Spirit is love, joy, peace, forbearance, kindness, goodness, faithfulness, gentleness and self-control. Against such things there is no law.

The NLT adds:

> But the Holy Spirit produces this kind of fruit in our lives: love, joy, peace, patience, kindness, goodness, faithfulness, gentleness, and self-control. There is no law against these things!

Furthermore, God's word is eternal. Luke 21:33 (NIV; see also Matt. 24:35; Mark 13:31) says:

> "Heaven and earth will pass away, but my words will never pass away."

1 Pet. 1:25a (AMP, BSB, CSA, ESV, GNT, GW, NIV, NKJV, NLT) adds:

> But the word of the Lord endures forever ... remains forever ... stands forever ... lasts forever.

Psa. 119:89 (BSB) notes:

> Your word, O Lord, is everlasting; it is firmly fixed in the heavens.

Verse 160 (NASB) of that chapter writes:

*The sum of your word is truth, And every one of your righteous ordinances is everlasting.*

Isa. 40:8 (ESV, NASB, NKJV) states:

*The grass withers, the flower fades, But the word of our God stands forever.*

Moreover, God's word is active, living and powerful. Jesus said in John 6:63 (NASB):

*"It is the Spirit who gives life; the flesh profits nothing; the words that I have spoken to you are spirit and are life."*

Heb. 4:12 (NKJV) notes:

*For the word of God is living and powerful, and sharper than any two-edged sword, piercing even to the division of soul and spirit, and of joints and marrow, and is a discerner of the thoughts and intents of the heart.*

Isa. 55:11 (TPT) writes:

*"So also will be the word that I speak; it does not return to me unfulfilled. My word performs my purpose and fulfills the mission I sent it out to accomplish."*

The Message translation of this verse adds:

*"So will the words that come out of my mouth not come back empty-handed. They'll do the work I sent them to do; they'll complete the assignment I gave them."*

Finally, God's word—both the logos and rhema—is inspired. 2 Tim 3:16 (NKJV) says:

*All Scripture is given by inspiration of God, and is profitable for doctrine, for reproof, for correction, for instruction in righteousness.*

The NIV adds:

*All Scripture is God-breathed and is useful for teaching, rebuking, correcting and training in righteousness.*

2 Pet. 1:21 (NKJV) writes:

*For prophecy never had its origin in the human will, but prophets, though human, spoke from God as they were carried along by the Holy Spirit.*

So, in sum, the royal law (love) and the word of God are superior to the laws of man.

# JURISDICTION

One additional, foundational legal concept must be defined and discussed at this point, as it applies to the Courts of Heaven, and that is jurisdiction. Jurisdiction is defined as the power, right and/or authority that an official of a court of law, government agency or regulatory body has to enforce laws, set a docket, assign judges to cases, administer hearings, try cases, determine and rule on what evidence is admissible, grant or deny motions and petitions, grant or refuse injunctions, interpret and apply local statutes and ordinances or the national constitution, issue verdicts and rulings and judgments, issue legal opinions, impose sentences, issue citations and fines, and/or carry out legal judgments.[8]

Thus, an important and basic question of law is whether a given court has jurisdiction to hear, preside over and adjudicate a given case. All earthly legal systems, governments and their agencies, regulatory bodies, courts and court officials have a limited, finite scope of operation and territorial, legal class, and/or subject matter boundaries in which to function and exercise authority. But, since God is the First Cause and Sovereign of the universe as Creator and Sustainer of all life, and the Supreme Judge of the living and the dead, His heavenly court system—the Courts of Heaven—has full jurisdiction over cases involving His sons and daughters, the saints of God/disciples of Christ.

The Courts of Heaven has jurisdiction to hear cases involving the saints or followers of Christ, since Jesus stated to His disciples, "All authority has been given to Me in heaven and on earth" (Matt. 28:18, NKJV). Scripture also states, "And if anyone sins, we have an Advocate with the Father, Jesus Christ the Righteous" (1 John 2:1, NKJV). Moreover, James 4:12 says, "There is only one Lawgiver and Judge, the One who is able to save and to destroy;..." Numerous other Scriptures also refer to Father God as the heavenly Judge of all and the Judge of the living and the dead (Dan. 7:9-10; Rom. 2:16; Heb. 9:27, 10:30, 12:22-24; James 5:9; 1 Pet. 4:5; Rev. 20:11-15). See also Gen. 1:27; Isa. 45:23; Matt. 22:17-22; Mark 12:15-17; Rom. 14:11; Col. 1:15-20; 1 Tim. 6:15; Rev. 17:14, 19:16.

There are several different types of legal jurisdiction on earth, including but not limited to Original Jurisdiction, Exclusive Jurisdiction, Personal Jurisdiction, Subject Matter Jurisdiction, General Jurisdiction, Specific Jurisdiction, Limited Jurisdiction, Territorial Jurisdiction, Concurrent Jurisdiction, and Appellate Jurisdiction. By way of application, I propose and assert that the

Courts of Heaven has Original Jurisdiction, Exclusive Jurisdiction, General Jurisdiction, Specific Jurisdiction, Personal Jurisdiction, Subject Matter Jurisdiction, Territorial Jurisdiction and Appellate Jurisdiction for the saints of God/disciples and followers of Christ. And occasionally, the Courts of Heaven may also have Concurrent Jurisdiction in cases where more than one heavenly Court is involved or has jurisdiction. The word Concurrent means shared or overlapping jurisdiction.[9]

# PRAYING FOR PROTECTION

Now that I have discussed legal standing, governing law, and jurisdiction as they apply to the Courts of Heaven, and laid a strong legal foundation to build upon, you are ready to proceed. I recommend that you or one of your team members, if any, pray a prayer of security and protection as you begin your session. I have found this to be extremely important and a necessary precaution. The purpose and goal of such a prayer is to protect you and any others who may be participating with you in the session, as well as your family, your home or residence and/or office or workplace, and any electronic equipment you may be using during the session—such as computers, tablets and/or phones—and to pray against and bind up any and all backlash and retaliation from our enemy, Satan, and the demonic spirits which serve him.

In heaven, God is surrounded and attended by legions and myriads of holy angels, and so your safety and security is not an issue there, in that dimension, but the earthly realm is an altogether different matter, and it is important that you pray for your physical safety and protection during the session, and that of your family, and any seers who may be assisting you, as well as your possessions and property, and theirs. Feel free to use your own words and pray from the heart as you are led by the Holy Spirit. If you would like to have a prayer template to help you with this prayer, or to give you some suggested prayer points, one is provided for you below.

# COH SECURITY PRAYER FOR AN INDIVIDUAL, GROUP OR ORGANIZATION

## PRAYER TEMPLATE:

Father God, in the name of Jesus, I/we set security for this Courts of Heaven session today.

I/We pray a canopy and hedge of protection over each and every person in this meeting, and all participants in this session. I/we decree an impenetrable, impregnable, divine dome of protection over and around us and our families today, completely enclosing, shielding and surrounding us.

I/We assign and release warrior angels and guardian angels and any other type and rank of angels needed for this session to surround the perimeter of this dome and monitor the atmosphere over this session. This dome is controlled by the angels of God and the heavenly host.

I/We assign a picket line of angels as well, and we bind up, cancel, disarm, nullify, and render powerless, harmless and useless, any and all backlash, retaliation and interference plans, strategies and attacks from the enemy, as well as any hitchhiker spirits, territorial spirits, and any other demonic spirits, in the name of Jesus.

I/We decree and declare divine protection over all of our electronic equipment and devices, software and systems, communication networks and platforms, and over our homes, offices, finances, health, physical bodies, emotions, voices, hearts and minds.

I/We decree divine encryption over everything that is spoken, seen, heard and/or shared during this session, and decree and declare that nothing from this session can be seen, heard, eavesdropped, wiretapped, lost, stolen, intercepted, delayed, hindered, interfered with, or decoded by the enemy in the natural realm, and that this dome is off limits to astral projection and other schemes, strategies, technologies, plans or devices of the enemy.

I/We decree the Lord God is our shield and defender. There is a no-fly zone ban and security protocol in force immediately and each person in this session is fully dressed, trained, equipped and armed for spiritual warfare.

I/We decree and declare no weapon formed against us shall prosper. I/We plead and apply the blood of Jesus to each person here. In the mighty name of Jesus, Amen.

# EPHESIANS 2:5-6

While for some readers one point may be obvious, and already understood, I believe it is important to point out for other readers who may not be familiar with this, that during your Courts of Heaven session, your body is on earth, but your spirit is in heaven. So, in the Spirit, you can be two places at once. I call this being bi-dimensional or bi-locational. The scriptural basis for this is found in Eph. 2:5-6, and we will review several different translations of this below for clarity and emphasis.

The New Living Translation (NLT, author's emphasis) states:

> [T]hat even though we were dead because of our sins, he gave us life when he raised Christ from the dead. (It is only by God's grace that you have been saved!) **For he raised us from the dead along with Christ and seated us with him in the heavenly realms because we are united with Christ Jesus.**

Note that the two verbs in this last sentence—raised and seated—are both past tense. They have already happened. But, we have to believe it and act on it.

The Passion Translation (TPT, author's emphasis) says:

> Even when we were dead and doomed in our many sins, he united us into the very life of Christ and saved us by his wonderful grace! **He raised us up with Christ the exalted One, and we ascended with him into the glorious perfection and authority of the heavenly realm, for we are now co-seated as one with Christ!**

Notice that "we ascended with him into the ... heavenly realm" and that "we are now co-seated ... with Christ." It's already happened.

The New King James Version (NKJV, author's emphasis) also notes:

> [E]ven when we were dead in trespasses, **[God] made us alive together with Christ** (by grace you have been

*saved), **and raised us up together, and made us sit together in the heavenly places in Christ Jesus.***

So, this brief sampling of translations shows that there is general and widespread agreement among translators on the meaning of these verses.[10]

But, we must exercise our faith by believing and acting upon this Scripture for it to benefit us in this life. And, since we know that Christ is seated on a throne in heaven at the right hand of God, we also have been seated there with Him in heaven; there are thrones that we can occupy in the realm of the Spirit.[11] We can choose to do this by faith at any time as the Spirit leads. However, it is certainly helpful if you have developed and learned to use your sanctified imagination. If not, there is a first time for everything, and now is a good time to start using that.

# CONSECRATE YOURSELF

Now that you have prayed for security and protection for your time in the Courts of Heaven, and bound up backlash and retaliation, the next step is for you to pray a prayer of consecration in observance of Psa. 24:3-6 (NIV):

*Who may ascend the mountain of the Lord? Who may stand in his holy place? The one who has clean hands and a pure heart, who does not trust in an idol or swear by a false god. They will receive blessing from the Lord and vindication from God their Savior. Such is the generation of those who seek him, who seek your face, God of Jacob.*

I invite and encourage you to be led by the Holy Spirit and pray a spontaneous prayer of personal consecration from your own heart. If, however, you feel you need or would like to use a prayer template to help you, one is provided for you below. If there is more than one Defendant in this session, then you can either pray the prayer below, and the subsequent prayers in later chapters, in unison, or one at a time, as you prefer. And, it is important that each Defendant pray each prayer aloud. However, if you have a pronounced speech impediment, are deaf or have significant hearing loss, or have a deaf mute condition, then God will know and understand that, and those individuals can just pray silently.

# CONSECRATION PRAYER

## PRAYER TEMPLATE:

Gracious Heavenly Father, I consecrate myself now to Your purposes and to Your will and plan for my life, O God, and I surrender and dedicate myself to You now, afresh and anew, and embrace Your plans and purposes for my life and the bright future that You have created and planned for me. I ask You to search the motives and intents of my heart, and to show me any anxious thoughts or wrong ways within me, and any blind spots and/or areas of my life that are not pleasing to You, and are not in harmony or agreement with Your word. I humble myself before You as I prepare to enter Your courts, and I pray that I may find mercy, favor and justice in Your sight. I empty myself so that You can fill me again.

I choose to lay aside and lay down every yoke, burden, care and weight that is not from You, and to rest in Your finished work and incomparable victory at the cross, and at the tomb. I thank You, Lord, that You said Your yoke is easy and Your burden is light, and that I can enter into Your rest, and work from a place of peace and rest. I invite You, Lord, to heal any tiredness, weariness, fatigue, illness, sickness, disease, disappointment, offense, wound, heartache, trauma, abuse, betrayal, rejection, and/or abandonment, in my body, soul, and spirit today, and to restore, refresh and replenish me, and make me brand new.

I thank You that I am born in the fullness of time for my destiny, and that with Your help, and by Your grace, wisdom and strength, I will fulfill and accomplish everything that You have planned and purposed for me to do in the earth. I lean not on my own understanding, but in all my ways I acknowledge You, and I thank You that I am fearfully and wonderfully made in Your image. I choose to trust You fully and completely in every area of my life to meet all of my needs from Your abundance, storehouses, treasuries and kingdom resources.

With the help of the Holy Spirit, I choose to walk in agreement with Your heart's desires for me and the plans You formed and wrote in my book in heaven before I was born. Like David of old, in Psalm 16:6 (CSB, HCS), I can say, "The boundary lines have fallen for me in pleasant places; indeed, I have a beautiful heritage."

# OPENING YOUR BOOK OF DESTINY

Next, it is necessary to pray for the book containing your purpose, destiny and identity to be opened in heaven, since you, and any seers who are with you, if any, will need access to your book while in the Courts of Heaven. This is mentioned in Psalm 139. You can pray a simple, spontaneous prayer from your heart for this, or if you feel you want or need some help or guidance, a prayer template is provided below to help you.

Psa. 139:15-16 says (NASB, author's emphasis):

*My frame was not hidden from You, When I was made in secret, And skillfully wrought in the depths of the earth;* **Your eyes have seen my unformed substance; And in Your book were all written The days that were ordained for me, When as yet there was not one of them.**

Your book in heaven is important enough to warrant citing other translations here for emphasis. The NIV (author's emphasis) adds:

*My frame was not hidden from you when I was made in the secret place, when I was woven together in the depths of the earth.* **Your eyes saw my unformed body; all the days ordained for me were written in your book before one of them came to be.**

Psa. 139:15-16 (NLT, author's emphasis) states:

*You watched me as I was being formed in utter seclusion, as I was woven together in the dark of the womb.* **You saw me before I was born. Every day of my life was recorded in your book. Every moment was laid out before a single day had passed.**

The Passion Translation (TPT, author's emphasis) writes:

*You even formed every bone in my body when you created me in the secret place, carefully, skillfully shaping me from nothing to something. **You saw who you created me to be before I became me! Before I'd ever seen the light of day, the number of days you planned for me were already recorded in your book.***

It's not just the quantity of days and time recorded in your book of destiny in heaven that matters, but of equal or greater importance is the quality of this precious time that God has ordained for you in the earth. As a wise steward, you will want to steward that time well and produce an abundant harvest and fruit that remains. It is this quality component that involves your purpose, destiny and identity that God has planned for your life; this will become part of the evidence presented in your defense, and the court record for your case in the Courts of Heaven. This is one of many reasons it is helpful, though not required, to have one or more seasoned seers as part of your session and legal defense team.

The prayer on the following page can either be read by you or one of your seers, if any, or your whole team of seers if you have more than one seer in the Courtroom with you.

# PRAYER TO OPEN YOUR BOOK IN HEAVEN

## PRAYER TEMPLATE:

I/We stand in agreement with the book of my/your life written in heaven by God before I/you was/were created or born. I/We ask that everything written there come to pass and be fulfilled in the fullness of time for my/your purpose and destiny, and I/ we pledge our cooperation to that end. I/We ask that my/your Counselor, Holy Spirit, obtain and produce before the Court all relevant records related to my/your case. I/We call for all entries that are contained in these records to be revealed and understood that affect me/you, my/your ancestral bloodline, and those joined to me/you by covenant. I/We request by faith according to Psalm 139 that the book of my/your life be opened now and revealed to me/you, and any seers with me/you, fully today. I/We further request that the full contents of my/your book of purpose and destiny be seen, revealed, understood, and expressed today. In the mighty name of Jesus, amen.

Finally, let's look for a moment at the books of remembrance. An excellent example of this is found in Mal. 3:16 (NASB, author's emphasis):

> Then those who feared the LORD spoke to one another, and the LORD gave attention and heard it, and **a book of remembrance was written before Him** for those who fear the LORD and who esteem His name.

Another great example of this is found in the Book of Esther, Chapter 6. Verses 1-3 (NIV, author's emphasis) read:

> That night the king could not sleep; so **he ordered the book of the chronicles, the record of his reign, to be brought in and read to him. It was found recorded there that Mordecai had exposed Bigthana and Teresh, two of the king's officers who guarded the doorway, who had conspired to assassinate King Xerxes.** "What

*honor and recognition has Mordecai received for this?"
the king asked. "Nothing has been done for him," his
attendants answered. So, the king then ordered Haman,
one of the chief princes, to honor Mordecai on his behalf,
and Haman did so, clothing Mordecai with a royal robe
and leading him on horseback through the city streets
while proclaiming before him, "This is what is done for
the man the king delights to honor!"*

# REMEMBRANCE PRAYER

## PRAYER TEMPLATE:

I/We ask that the words spoken today in my/your case and
session in the Courts of Heaven, be recorded in a book of
remembrance before the Lord just as it was done in Malachi
3:16: "Then those who feared the LORD spoke to one another,
and the LORD gave attention and heard it, and a book of
remembrance was written before Him for those who fear the
LORD and who esteem His name."

Now that your preparation has been completed for the Courts
of Heaven, we turn our attention to Chapter 3.

## ENDNOTES

1. See Ezek. 11:19, 36:26; Jer. 31:33; Luke 6:31; John 15:12; Gal. 6:2, 10; Heb. 8:10; 1 John 3:18.

2. Definition is from Wikipedia. https://en.wikipedia.org/wiki/Standing_(law)

3. Definition is from the online *Merriam-Webster Dictionary*. https://www.merriam-webster.com/dictionary/common-law

4. https://en.wikipedia.org/wiki/List_of_national_legal_systems

5. Definitions are from the online *Cambridge Dictionary*. https://dictionary.cambridge.org/us/dictionary/english/civil-law

6. https://en.wikipedia.org/wiki/List_of_national_legal_systems

7. Ibid.

8. https://en.wikipedia.org/wiki/Jurisdiction, https://www.merriam-webster.com/dictionary/jurisdiction, https://dictionary.cambridge.org/us/dictionary/english/jurisdiction, https://www.britannica.com/topic/jurisdiction

9. https://www.law.cornell.edu/wex/jurisdiction, https://en.wikipedia.org/wiki/Jurisdiction, https://www.britannica.com/topic/jurisdiction

10. The Courts of Heaven are located in the Third Heaven dimension or heavenly realm, where God, Jesus, the holy angels, the 24 elders, the four living creatures and the great Cloud of Witnesses dwell. I am aware of Rev. 21:27 which says that nothing impure or defiled shall enter there, referring to the eternal city, Mt. Zion or the New Jerusalem. I believe in context this verse is referring to the saints who enter into the eternal city in heaven permanently, for eternity, after the Great White Throne judgment. That verse specifically mentions "only those whose names are written in the Lamb's book of life." There are also "heavenly places" outside of the eternal city. So, regardless of exactly where this Courtroom activity takes place, it is in the Third Heaven dimension. I have cited Heb. 12:22-24 and Eph. 2:5-6 several times in the book in support of this, as well as Dan.l 7:9-10. Satan has a legal right to be there in some but not all of the Courts of Heaven as a temporary visitor, even though he has been evicted permanently as a resident, and his heavenly citizenship has been revoked, canceled and nullified long ago by God.

11. For a fuller treatment and discussion of the subject of thrones in Scripture, please refer to Dr. Gordon E. Bradshaw, 2015, *I See Thrones! Igniting & Increasing Your Influence in the Seven Mountains of Culture*, Lakebay, WA: Kingdom House Publishing. See also Rev. 20:4-6.

## CHAPTER 3
# ENTERING THE COURTS OF HEAVEN

Now that you are ready to enter the Courts of Heaven, you will be referred to as a "Defendant." If there is more than one Defendant with you in this case, you will be referred to collectively as "Defendants." By way of disclaimer, I ask you to suspend whatever you know or think you know about how courts and the legal system operate and function during this session, and as you read and apply the rest of this book. This is heaven, and God is omnipotent, omnipresent and omniscient. He writes, interprets and applies the laws and rules as He sees fit.

While there are some similarities with earthly courts and legal systems, there is definitely not a direct or 1 to 1 correlation. In fact, there is a big difference, because in heaven we are in the realm of the Spirit, and therefore, many of the same limitations that we have on earth in our human bodies, and in the legal system itself, don't apply to the court system in heaven. Furthermore, the governing law, some of the rules of legal procedure, and the ordering and sequencing of events in the Courts, are quite different.

Also, my focus in this book in terms of dialogue in the Courts is on Defendants, so I have not recorded or explained every action or statement of the Plaintiff(s) (Satan and his henchmen), the Prosecuting Attorney (Satan), the Defense Attorney (Jesus, your Advocate), and the Judge (God). To do so would be cumbersome, lengthy, and unnecessary. However, I have explained in great detail the role and function of each of these. My goal here is not to produce a trial transcript, but to help you to systematically and comprehensively deal with and resolve the outstanding sin issues in your ancestral bloodline, by following the Holy Spirit and reading prayers of identificational repentance that will help bring relief, freedom and breakthrough from Satanic and demonic influence in your life and family.

**YOU DON'T HAVE TO WAIT MONTHS OR YEARS FOR YOUR CASE TO COME TO TRIAL OR TO MEET WITH GOD.** Things happen at accelerated speed and in real time in the Courts of Heaven with motions, subpoenas, and other legal procedures, and there is no court calendar or court docket to try and get scheduled on, so you don't have to wait months or years for your case to come to trial or to meet with God. And, God has myriads of holy angels to help Him rather than law clerks. This Court venue for families, couples and individuals is a bench trial, where the judge presides and decides the verdict and makes the ruling, and there is no jury. Trials can happen in a matter of hours, not weeks, months or years. God can be many places at once, and can move at the speed of light, or faster. So can Jesus. And, so can the Holy Spirit. This levels the playing field for the saints of God and makes it very easy for God's children to access the Courts of Heaven.

# THE HEAVENLY COURT SYSTEM

I am sometimes asked this question: "Which Court will my session be held in?" There is an easy answer to that, which is: Pray and let the Holy Spirit decide which Court is appropriate for your case, and let the Holy Spirit lead and guide you there. It's definitely not something to stress over, be anxious about, or try to overanalyze or wrap your brain around. It's just one detail among many, and it's either discerned by the Spirit or it's not. I take a more pragmatic or practical approach to this question than some, and let the Holy Spirit take the lead on that. Some people have told me they get frustrated because they have either too little information, or too much information, about the Courts of Heaven. Please relax and enjoy the process, and let the Holy Spirit take the wheel and drive.

That question also suggests at least one other question, which is, "How many Courts are there in heaven?" All I will say about this for now is that Scripture is silent on this point and I have visited several different Courts in heaven. I haven't fully investigated this because I have simple childlike faith, and because I stay fairly busy leading sessions for families, individuals and couples; we seem to always be in the same Court for those type of sessions. Occasionally, I lead sessions for organizations in the Courts of Heaven, and then we seem to be in a different Court venue for those sessions. I have led or co-led sessions for several cities and nations as well, and those also seem to involve a different Court.

Some Courts in heaven have bench trials, with a single Judge presiding; that is true for your case, and that Judge is God. Other Courts and cases involve nations, and these may often have a tribunal Court presiding, such as is used by the military, where a panel of military officers from the same branch of service, comprises the tribunal for a trial. One example of this is found in Dan. 7:9-10 (NLT):

> I watched as thrones were put in place and the Ancient One sat down to judge. His clothing was as white as snow, his hair like purest wool. He sat on a fiery throne with wheels of blazing fire, and a river of fire was pouring out, flowing from his presence. Millions of angels ministered to him; many millions stood to attend him. Then the court began its session, and the books were opened.

Thrones symbolize rank and authority. They are seats of power and authority for governing, ruling and enforcing the will of a king and kingdom. Thrones being set in place implies and suggests a tribunal Court in this passage. The Hebrew word used for "thrones" is *karesawan*, from the root *korse*, meaning: "a throne." The Hebrew word used for "court" in verse 10, as well as in verse 27, is *wedina*, from the root *din*, meaning: "judgment, court, just."[1]

Later in that chapter, it says in verses 21-27 (NLT):

> As I watched, this horn was waging war against God's holy people and was defeating them, until the Ancient

*One—the Most High—came and judged in favor of his holy people. Then the time arrived for the holy people to take over the kingdom. Then He said to me, "This fourth beast is the fourth world power that will rule the earth. It will be different from all the others. It will devour the whole world, trampling and crushing everything in its path. Its ten horns are ten kings who will rule that empire.*

*Then another king will arise, different from the other ten, who will subdue three of them. He will defy the Most High and oppress the holy people of the Most High. He will try to change their sacred festivals and laws, and they will be placed under his control for a time, times, and half a time. But then the court will pass judgment, and all his power will be taken away and completely destroyed. Then the sovereignty, power, and greatness of all the kingdoms under heaven will be given to the holy people of the Most High. His kingdom will last forever, and all rulers will serve and obey him.*

This Court in Daniel 7 appears to be a tribunal Court with multiple judges, but with God as the presiding judge. God judged in favor of His holy people, the saints, in verse 21. But, in verse 26, it says that *"the court will pass judgment."* This suggests a Council of Judges for this Court of Nations, made up of those who exercise and steward significant authority and trust from God, and who have been invited to join His ruling Council in heaven, and to participate in discussions and decisions which will affect the earth, nations, and/or the Church. Robert Henderson calls this realm "standing in the Counsel of the Lord."[2]

When this Court passes judgment, notice in verse 27 that there is a timing component involved in their judicial decision, and that political, power and economic/financial structures in nations shift dramatically as a result in favor of the Church, or Ecclesia. It's no wonder, then, that God sits in heaven and laughs and scoffs at those who mock Him and His Son, Jesus Christ, in Psa. 2:4. He also rebukes and terrifies them and warns them to serve the Lord with holy fear and to celebrate His rule, in verses 5 and 10. And, in verse 12, the rulers of the earth are strongly advised and warned to kiss or embrace His Son.

Several years ago I was recognized and appointed as a Magistrate in the Courts of Heaven to help guide others, and I received a mandate. I believe there are other ranks and positions for those God chooses and appoints to help Him rule and govern the affairs of nations from the Council in heaven. I have met a few senior leaders who have told me they are a part of that Council. Be open to these and other assignments in heaven's Courts if God asks or invites you. You can have assignments from God both on earth and in heaven—by and in the Spirit—that are part of your destiny. And, as a point of information for those who may have interest, I have included in a footnote at the end of this chapter, the names and resources of some of those who have attempted to map or diagram the Heavenly Court System.[3]

# TRANSITION AND ASCEND IN THE SPIRIT INTO HEAVEN

Now, you are ready to transition and ascend in the Spirit into heaven by faith. Refer back to our earlier discussion about Eph. 2:5-6 in Chapter 2, as or if needed. I recommend that you pray a spontaneous prayer from the heart now to help you transition and ascend in the Spirit into heaven. And, for those who would like to have a prayer template to help them with this prayer, or to give them some suggested prayer points, one is provided for you below.

# TRANSITION PRAYER

## PRAYER TEMPLATE:

I/We come to these proceedings in the name of and through the Blood of Jesus and His righteousness.

I/We request access and that the Courts of Heaven be opened to me/us now by faith and through our legal standing in Jesus.

I/We now come up or ascend in spirit with clean hands and pure hearts according to Psalm 24:3-6 and Ephesians 2:6. (pause for a moment as needed)

I/We enter Your gates with thanksgiving and Your Courts with praise. I/We worship You, Lord, in spirit and in truth. (pause for a moment as needed)

I/We am/are now entering the Courts of Heaven! (pause for a moment as needed)

I/We recognize the presence and glory of the Lord is here with me/us now! (pause for a moment as needed)

I/We come before Father God, who in the Courts of Heaven is the impartial, Supreme Judge of all creation.

I/We honor Father, Son and Holy Spirit, as well as the holy angels, and the great Cloud of Witnesses.

I/We thank You Father God for granting me/us mercy and justice today in the Courts of Heaven. Amen.

# SETTING THE SCENE

Pause briefly if you need a moment to compose yourself or adjust to being in the heavenly realm, or to orient yourself in the Courts of Heaven. Typically, my team and I see Father God seated at the bench with a gavel in front of Him. The bench is a raised platform enclosed on three sides that is slightly higher than the tables on both sides of the Courtroom for opposing counsel. The area where you and Jesus are seated on one side of the Court is known in legal terms as the bar. Your legal team, if you have any seers with you, is seated next to you.

Satan is also seated at the bar across the room at a different table with his henchmen. There are holy angels present, who function as the bailiffs and courtroom reporters, and also warrior angels for security. In the gallery are often seated some members of the great Cloud of Witnesses. When you are ready to proceed, then read aloud the opening statement below.

## OPENING STATEMENT PRAYER TEMPLATE:

I/We am/are here today on behalf of [name of Defendant(s)] to help present my/our defense in the case being brought against me/us by the archenemy of my/our soul, Satan, and his demonic henchmen.

(If you have any prophetic seers with you in the Courtroom, please add:) These seers are part of my/<u>name of Defendant's</u> legal team and are here to assist me/Defendant(s) in these legal proceedings.

Jesus is my/our Advocate and Defender in this case. His righteousness and blood cover me/us and speak on my/our behalf. I/We look forward to the opportunity to face my/our Accuser(s), and to hear the charges and evidence against me/us. And, I/we throw myself/ourselves on the mercy of the Court. I/We am/are confident that after all of the evidence and testimony have been presented and reviewed in my/our case, and after my/our prayers of repentance have been heard and entered into the record, and any outstanding sins and/or curses in my/our ancestral bloodline have been forgiven and canceled, that I/we will be found Not Guilty of the charges against me/us, and that the charges will be dismissed. I/We thank You, Father God, for hearing and ruling upon my/our case today in the Courts of Heaven.

# PRESENTING YOUR CASE BEFORE GOD, THE SUPREME JUDGE

Isa. 43:26 (NKJV) declares:

> *"Put Me in remembrance; Let us contend together; State your case, that you may be acquitted."*

That's about as straightforward as it gets. This is God inviting His people through the prophet Isaiah to put Him in remembrance of their covenant relationship with Him, and their faithfulness and good deeds, and to contend or reason with God as Jacob and Job did. God is inviting His people to repent of their sins and state or present their case before Him with the goal of being acquitted and declared not guilty. You and I can do the same thing today, and the best and safest place to do that is in the Courts of Heaven. We have both Jesus as our Advocate and the Holy Spirit available and willing to help us.

We know that only judges and/or juries acquit Defendants, so we will briefly examine God's role as Judge. This is one very important facet or aspect of His nature and function as the Creator, Sustainer, and Sovereign, Supreme Being of the universe. He oversees the Courts of Heaven as well as the universe. And, we can access God now, not just in the future in eternity.

Isa. 33:22 (CSB, HCS) says:

> For the Lord is our judge, the Lord is our lawgiver, the Lord is our King. He will save us.

Jas. 4:12 (BSB) adds:

> There is only one Lawgiver and Judge, the One who is able to save and destroy. But you—who are you to judge your neighbor?

And Heb. 12:22-24 (ESV) states:

> But you have come to Mount Zion and to the city of the living God, the heavenly Jerusalem, and to innumerable angels in festal gathering, and to the assembly of the firstborn who are enrolled in heaven, and to God, the judge of all, and to the spirits of the righteous made perfect,and to Jesus, the mediator of a new covenant, and to the sprinkled blood that speaks a better word than the blood of Abel.

Finally, Dan. 7:9-10 (NLT) paints a remarkable and unforgettable picture of God as Judge:

> I watched as thrones were put in place and the Ancient One sat down to judge. His clothing was as white as snow, his hair like purest wool. He sat on a fiery throne with wheels of blazing fire, and a river of fire was pouring out, flowing from his presence. Millions of angels ministered to him; many millions stood to attend him. Then the court began its session, and the books were opened.

Notice that God is referred to in these Scriptures as the only Lawgiver and Judge, the One who can save and destroy, and as the Ancient of Days. He was seated on a flaming, fiery throne, with a river of fire flowing out from before Him, and millions of angels attending Him. This is not just any old judge! This is the preeminent Judge of the entire universe, of both the living and the dead. 1 Pet. 4:5 (NLT) reads:

> But remember that they will have to face God, who stands ready to judge everyone, both the living and the dead.

God is not only the Supreme Judge, but the Lawgiver, the One who wrote the very laws that form the legal basis for cases, trials, courts and court systems, justice, and righteousness. Moreover, this same Judge can be addressed by us outside of Court as Abba! In Court, He must be fair and impartial to fulfill His role with integrity and objectivity and remain true to His nature. Outside of Court, we are His children and He is our loving Father.

But, there is no conflict of interest or bias or nepotism on His part in hearing and ruling on your case as Judge, and so He has no need to recuse Himself from your case! He not only writes the laws as the Lawgiver, but He follows and abides by the laws, and the rules of His heavenly court system. He is the Judge above all judges and He has no equal! Furthermore, the foundations of His throne are righteousness and justice.[4]

And, you are here before Him now, seated next to Jesus your Advocate in the Courts of Heaven. Take a few moments and present a brief summary of your case to Him, with the help of Jesus and your legal team of seers, if any. Give Him your side of the story. And, ask Him for justice to be granted in your case. Take a few moments now and do that in your own words. Pause here for as much time as needed, typically from 5 to 30 minutes.

I have found that anything beyond 30 minutes here is probably excessive, and may even be counterproductive. This is not a pity party, and it is not a time to nurse and rehearse all of your hurts, wounds, offenses, pain, trauma and drama. You are in a Courtroom before the Living God of the universe and you need to speak wisely, humbly, boldly, concisely and succinctly, from the heart and by the Spirit, and allow your defense team to help you. Jesus your Advocate may have some suggestions for you.

This is your opportunity to tell God, and your prophetic seers, if any, about yourself and your situation. Share your story and what issues or circumstances you would like to address and resolve. State why you have asked for a Courts of Heaven session(s), and what you would like God the Judge and His holy angels to do for you in the Courts of Heaven, and share anything you want to remind Him of and bring to His attention and remembrance. Remind Him of injustices against you, and any prophecies or dreams you have received about your purpose and destiny, and anything written in your book in heaven. If you would like to have a prayer template to help you with this prayer, or to give you some suggested prayer points, one is provided for you below.

# PRESENTING A BRIEF SUMMARY OF YOUR CASE

## PRAYER TEMPLATE:

Father God, I am here today to repent for my sins and for the sins of my ancestral bloodline and those joined to us by covenant. I am also here to face my accusers, and to address and respond to the charges and accusations brought against me, and the evidence held against me, by Satan and his henchmen and demonic horde. Jesus, my Advocate, will be defending me today in these proceedings. His blood was shed for me and covers me and speaks for me on my behalf. His righteousness gives me right standing to appear in this Court, Your Honor, and to plead my case. Your Honor, I remind You that I am a joint heir with Jesus, and that I am a partaker of His covenant. My prophecies and what is written in my book in heaven, and what is written in Your word, speak a different reality and existence than what I have been experiencing so far, and I want to change. I contend for the fullness and the fulfillment of these words of prophecy and life spoken to and written about me, to come to pass quickly and to manifest in my life without any further delay, hindrance, interference, resistance or opposition from the enemy of my soul, Satan, and his demons. I remind You, Lord, that I have been faithful and obedient, and have used my gifts and resources to bless and encourage others, and to expand and advance Your kingdom. I am contending with You today for a bright and amazing future. I want to do the greater works that Jesus mentioned in John 14:12, and I want to finish well, fulfill my purpose and destiny, and leave a godly legacy and inheritance for my family and friends. Holy Spirit, please reveal to me and/or my legal team the roots of any demonic influence, hindrance, delay, interference, resistance, blockage or opposition in either me or my ancestral bloodline, or those joined to us by covenant. I ask You specifically, Your Honor, to help me address, resolve and/or overcome the issues and challenges that I am facing and/or dealing with today. In Jesus' name, amen. (List any and all issues and challenges that you are facing currently and speak them into the record).

Author's Note: See Appendix B on page 249 for an additional opening prayer you can pray now if desired, but it is optional.

# ISSUING AND SERVING SUBPOENAS TO COMPEL DEMONIC SPIRITS TO APPEAR IN THE COURTS OF HEAVEN

As you are seated here in the Courts of Heaven next to Jesus at the defense table on one side of the Courtroom, and are preparing to hear and/or see the evidence Satan and his fallen angels/demonic spirits have been using against you and your family from your ancestral bloodline, there is something I recommend you and/or your legal team do procedurally at this point that is very powerful in the spirit realm.

ENTERING THE COURTS OF HEAVEN | 63

I have seen this Spirit-birthed petition that follows be extremely effective in causing large numbers of demonic spirits assigned to an ancestral bloodline to be brought into the Courtroom quickly and en masse, where you and Jesus and any seers who are with you, can then face the Accuser and his henchmen and underlings that are affecting or afflicting you through your ancestral bloodline. Just read the petition below out loud now, or ask one of your seers, if any, to do that for you on your behalf, and then in the Spirit, use your sanctified imagination to see Jesus hand this petition to the Judge after it is read. Typically, a large number of demonic spirits (usually tens of thousands) will be brought into the Courtroom at this point by the holy angels, along with any relevant evidence they possess that relates to your case.

## SUBPOENAS PETITION PRAYER TEMPLATE:

Your Honor, I/we petition this Court of Heaven to issue subpoenas and compel to appear any and all demonic spirits that relate to these legal proceedings and to this Defendant/these Defendants and their ancestral bloodline(s), and those joined to them by covenant. I/We ask that these subpoenas be served immediately in the spirit realm by You, Lord, the Supreme Judge, or by Your holy angels, and that these demonic spirits be compelled to bring with them any and all evidence they may have which relates to this bloodline/these bloodlines, this Defendant/these Defendants and/or this case. And, I/we further request that these demonic spirits (demons or fallen angels) of various ranks (thrones, dominions, principalities and powers) and authority, be chained and bound and disposed of according to Your will, O God, and with Your permission, be cast into the Abyss, according to Luke 8:26-39, Jude 1:6 and 2 Peter 4:4. In Jesus' mighty and glorious name, amen.

# DEMONIC SPIRITS

Within a few seconds of reading and presenting this petition to the Supreme Judge, Father God, and having it be approved and enacted, typically a large number of demonic spirits will appear and enter the Courtroom en masse and be seated on the Devil's side of the Courtroom. Typically, my ministry team and I see tens of thousands of demonic spirits come into the Courtroom in most sessions. But, if the Defendant has previously done some prayer work in the areas of repentance, forgiveness, inner healing, and/ or ancestral bloodline cleansing, then a lesser number of demons will appear in the Courtroom. We have not yet met any Defendant who was 100% clean spiritually and had no demonic spirits in their ancestral bloodline.

These demonic spirits are dealt with in stages, or sequentially, during the session by the holy angels as Defendant(s) reads the Prayers of Repentance listed in Chapters 6-15. Your heartfelt and sincere repentance cancels and removes the Devil's legal right to accuse, attack, harass, hinder, intimidate, influence, oppose, oppress and/or torment you through your ancestral bloodline. After each prayer is read by Defendant(s), we see demonic spirits that are assigned to and have been affecting those specific areas of the bloodline, being chained and bound and forcibly removed from the Courtroom by the holy angels, and cast into the Abyss.

Sometimes, we see Father God, the Judge, point at certain spirits as they are being removed, and these are banished to the

Abyss. The word for "abyss" in Greek is *abysson*, which is from the root *abussos*, meaning "bottomless pit."[5] In a recent session where we saw a large number of demons in the Defendant's ancestral bloodline, we saw several thousand demons chained and bound and removed from the Courtroom after Defendant read and prayed the prayer of repentance for sins of Religion. Such is the effect and power of your repentance in the Courts of Heaven.

The other prayers of repentance in this book have a similar effect on the demons assigned to your ancestral bloodline, but this obviously varies by Defendant and bloodline, as some bloodlines have more demons assigned to certain areas of sin than to others. So, while the enemy tries to put on a show of force in the Court, it is merely a charade and an act. The demons are in fact, in fear and trembling to stand before God as the Judge, no matter their rank. Jas. 2:19 (NLT) says:

> *You say you have faith, for you believe that there is one God. Good for you! Even the demons believe this, and they tremble in terror.*

Demons with higher rank are as a group commonly called or referred to as "strong man" spirits. This is from the use of that phrase in the Gospels of Matthew, Mark and Luke, in which they record the Parable of the Strong Man. Matt. 12:29 (NIV) says:

> *"Or again, how can anyone enter a strong man's house and carry off his possessions unless he first ties up the strong man? Then he can plunder his house."*

Luke 11:21-22 (NIV) adds:

> *"When a strong man, fully armed, guards his own house, his possessions are safe. But when someone stronger attacks and overpowers him, he takes away the armor in which the man trusted and divides up his plunder."*

The word "armor" here is from the Greek word *panoplian*, which is from the root word *panoplia*, meaning "a complete set of defensive and offensive armor (weapons); i.e., everything needed to wage successful warfare." It's the same word that Paul used in Eph. 6:11 (BSB, CSB, NASB, NIV), *"Put on the full armor of God ..."*[6] I believe Jesus is saying in this parable that while Satan is a strong opponent or adversary, he is overconfident and is trusting in faulty or flawed armor. The word "overpower" in Luke 11:22 is also translated "overcome." It's the Greek word *nikēsē* and is from the root *nikaó*, meaning to conquer, overcome, prevail, subdue. It's the same root word used in 1 John 5:4-5 and Rev. 12:11.[7] That is good news for the saints of God, and a vital piece of strategic information and intelligence that we can exploit and use to our advantage.

# SPIRITUAL HIERARCHY

Spiritual hierarchy or rank among demons is referred to several times in Scripture, using similar terms. The context of Eph. 6:12 is spiritual warfare with the demonic realm. Most translations agree on the terms used here, with the NIV citing *"rulers, authorities, powers of this dark world, and spiritual forces of evil in the heavenly realms"*; and other slight variations including *"rulers, authorities, cosmic or world powers of darkness, and spiritual forces of evil in the heavenly places or realms"* (ESV, BSB, CSB, HCS, GW). So, there is agreement among many translations on the language of this verse. The KJV and NKJV translations differ somewhat from this; they translate these terms *"principalities, powers, rulers of the darkness of this age, and spiritual hosts of wickedness in the heavenly places."*

A related passage in Col. 1:15-17 (MSG, author's emphasis) is a bit more complex and says:

> We look at this Son and see the God who cannot be seen. We look at this Son and see God's original purpose in everything created. For everything, absolutely everything, above and below, visible and invisible, **rank after rank after rank of angels**—everything got started in him and finds its purpose in him. He was there before any of it came into existence and holds it all together right up to this moment.

Regardless of the titles or positions described here, the MSG translator correctly perceived and understood that verse 16 is talking about spiritual rank among the angels—both the fallen angels and the holy angels. And, rank signifies authority, both in the natural realm and the spiritual realm. See Acts 19:11-20 for an example of that.

It is also important to point out here that angels are created beings. They are included in the phrase "everything created" in verse 15, and are subject to Christ in heaven. The first two chapters of Hebrews emphasize the superiority of Jesus over the angels in great detail, and Luke 20:35-36 makes the point that angels do not die. They are created spirit beings. Christ was in the beginning with Father God and preceded the angels in existence, and was present for their creation, and participated in it. John 1:3 (BSB) says:

68 | PRAYERS FOR CLEANSING ANCESTRAL BLOODLINES IN THE COURTS OF HEAVEN

> *Through Him all things were made, and without Him nothing was made that has been made.*

Heb. 1:2 (BSB) adds:

> *But in these last days He has spoken to us by His Son, whom He appointed heir of all things, and through whom He made the universe.*

The AMP, BSB, ESV, HCS, NASB and NIV translate Col. 1:16 as "*thrones or dominions or rulers or authorities.*" The NIV says, "*thrones or powers or rulers or authorities.*" The NLT says, "*thrones, kingdoms, rulers and authorities.*" The KJV and NKJV say, "*thrones or dominions or principalities or powers.*" So, rulers are synonymous with principalities, and authorities are synonymous with powers in this verse.

Similarly, Eph. 1:20-21 (BSB) says:

> *Which He exerted in Christ when He raised Him from the dead and seated Him at His right hand in the heavenly realms, far above all rule and authority, power and dominion, and every name that is named, not only in this age, but also in the one to come.*

The AMP, BSB, CSB, ESV, NASB, and NIV translate Eph. 1:21 as "*rule and authority, power and dominion.*" The KJV and NKJV say "*principality and power and might and dominion.*" So, these three Scriptures each mention four levels or types or ranks of authority in the angelic realm, and in the demonic kingdom.

I also want to mention here that demons have the ability to shape-shift and can appear in several different forms. Most often they appear in animal form in the Courtroom, but also can appear as half human-half animal (as in Baphomet and Ganesh), as fallen angels, or as humans.

Among the demonic forms we have seen in the Courtroom include bats, witches, wizards, warlocks, sorcerers, ogres, dragons, alligators, crocodiles, octopuses, sharks, snakes of various species, bears, wolves, foxes, tigers, cougars, pumas, panthers, the Grim Reaper (the spirit of death), humanlike creatures with horns and/or tails, coyotes, hyenas, jackals, buzzards, vultures, scorpions, spiders, rats, mice, Hell's Angels gang members (enforcers), religious spirits, figures wearing clerical robes, and even entities that try to disguise themselves by wearing trench coats, hats and sunglasses. These latter are often higher ranking demonic entities.

2 Cor. 11:14-15 (ESV) says:

> And no wonder, for even Satan disguises himself as an angel of light. So it is no surprise if his servants, also, disguise themselves as servants of righteousness. Their end will correspond to their deeds.

The NIV states:

> And no wonder, for Satan himself masquerades as an angel of light. It is not surprising, then, if his servants also masquerade as servants of righteousness. Their end will be what their actions deserve.

And the NKJV adds:

> And no wonder! For Satan himself transforms himself into an angel of light. Therefore it is no great thing if his ministers also transform themselves into ministers of righteousness, whose end will be according to their works.

The Greek word that is translated here variously as disguises, masquerades and transforms, is the verb *metaschématizó*, which means "to change in fashion or appearance outwardly; transfigure."[8] We know that Satan is jealous of God and tries to counterfeit the real, genuine, and authentic in God's kingdom, and to copy or reproduce that in his kingdom of darkness. Everything there is the opposite of God's kingdom, which is built on a gospel of good news; a mission to deliver, heal, set the captives free, open the eyes of the blind, and relieve the oppressed; and the principles and tenets of agape love and truth, faith and hope, righteousness and justice, peace and joy, order and clarity, unity and humility, strength and courage, freedom and life.

# THE KINGDOM OF DARKNESS

Satan's kingdom is built on hate and lies, disorder and confusion, strife and discord, evil and injustice, turmoil and chaos, fear and depression, doubt and unbelief, worry and anxiety, bondage and death. Satan has a counterfeit gospel of bad news, a counterfeit mission to kill, steal and destroy, counterfeit communion and sacraments, counterfeit priests and ministers, counterfeit signs and wonders, a counterfeit throne, counterfeit gifts and prophecies, a counterfeit altar and sacrifices, counterfeit worship, counterfeit leaders and generals, and fallen angels.

Satan is a legalist and he uses sins, iniquities, transgressions, curses, lies, and legal evidence from your ancestral bloodline against you. He is both a powerful and pitiful foe, a dangerous and defeated enemy, and a cunning and convicted adversary, as well as a deceiver, liar and accuser. He is a legalist precisely because he is uncomfortable with and was not satisfied by grace, and he rejected God's grace long ago.

Satan would rather rail against God and His word than repent. His pride, ambition, stubbornness, and lawless, rebellious, disgusting, despicable, deceptive, evil, vile, violent nature will not allow that. That's why your repentance is so effective against him in the Courts of Heaven; it has a devastating effect on the enemy's charges and evidence against you. Satan is void of humility and truth, is incorrigible, and is like those apostates spoken of in 1 Tim. 4:2 (NLT):

> These people are hypocrites and liars, and their consciences are dead.

The NIV says:

> Such teachings come through hypocritical liars, whose consciences have been seared as with a hot iron.

And, certainly, Satan is the chief angelic apostate who once led a third of the angels in heaven to rebel and sin and war with him against God, the Creator and Sustainer of all life.[9]

# YOUR ROLE IN PRAYER IS CRUCIAL

The contrast between these two kingdoms is clear, undeniable and unmistakable. Therefore, your role of standing in the gap for your family and your ancestral bloodline through authentic, genuine, heartfelt, Spirit-led, comprehensive and systematic repentance, is of critical importance and will make an important and decisive difference in your future. And, it will have a positive effect on your family as well, whether or not they are even aware of your repentance for your sins and the sins of your ancestral bloodline, and those joined to your bloodline by covenant. At this point, you are now ready to proceed with the evidentiary part of the legal proceedings in the Courts of Heaven, which we will discuss and describe next in some detail in Chapter 4.

**Author's Note:** It is important to point out here that by requesting the Subpoenas Petition to be granted in your case, which was mentioned earlier in this chapter on pages 63-64, and the Judge granting that Petition, this Petition overrules legally any real or imagined "Statute of Limitations" regarding how far back in time and/or how many generations back in your ancestral bloodline that demonic spirits on assignment against you or your family or with evidence relevant to your case can be accessed by the holy angels. This Petition is careful to leave that decision about ancestral timelines up to Father God, the Supreme Judge. Thus, my team and I find no need to mention or discuss any ancestral timeline in our Courts of Heaven sessions. We leave that decision up to Father God, the Supreme Judge, and focus our efforts, spiritual gifts and authority on helping Defendant(s) repent and deal with whatever number, type and rank of demonic spirits the holy angels bring into the Courtroom that have been served subpoenas by the Courts of Heaven and compelled to appear in your case.

Furthermore, even in earthly courts in certain jurisdictions, such as the federal courts in the U.S., and a few states, some felony crimes such as murder, war crimes, rape, sexual assault, sexual assault of a child, and aggravated criminal sexual assault have no Statute of Limitations.[10]

## ENDNOTES

1.  Strong's Hebrew, 3764, 1780.

2.  See Robert Henderson, *Prayers & Declarations That Open The Courts of Heaven*, 2018, Shippensburg, PA: Destiny Image Publishers, Inc., Chapter 4, "Operating as a Judge." See also Robert Henderson, *Praying for the Prophetic Destiny of the United States and The Presidency of Donald J. Trump From The Courts of Heaven*, 2020, Shippensburg, PA: Destiny Image Publishers, Inc., Chapter 3, "Standing in the Counsel of the Lord." See also Rick Joyner, *The Final Quest*, 1997, New Kensington, PA: Whitaker House and Dr. Luc Niebergall, *The Heart of Heaven: A Prophetic Encounter*, 2023, Calgary, AB Canada: The Author.

3.  The efforts of those who have tried to map or diagram the Heavenly Court System, are listed below as a resource for readers. This may not be a complete list, and is compiled using best efforts. While well intentioned and prophetic, such efforts have not always been well received by some in the body of Christ. There are a number of reasons for this.

    First, many in the body of Christ are not prophetic, and may not see or hear in the Spirit, and have not been taught, trained or activated in this, or developed these areas through usage. Some in this category may have cessationist views theologically, and do not believe in the gifts of the Holy Spirit being active and available today.

    Second, the number of Heavenly Courts proposed by these authors may be overwhelming to some people, who may struggle to process, understand and/or apply this information, or find these Courts not named in Scripture.

    Third, those who have diagrammed the Heavenly Court System may not be as well known to the body of Christ globally as some other ministers, and therefore may not be trusted by some to be stewards of such revelation. And, fourth, the respective diagrams put forth by these ministers, do not always match or line up exactly, although three or four ministers cited here use many of the same names for the Courts they list.

    God says in Scripture that He will establish a thing at the mouth of two or three witnesses. One minister proposes seven main Courts, with five more Courts within one of those; three other ministers propose 11 Courts; and a fifth minister has identified 15 Courts, although several of these fit within the same 11 cited by others. There may be other sources I am unaware of, but these are the ones I am familiar with, and they are enough to make my point. Some of the Courts proposed have different names and jurisdictions and organizational structures by the different authors, but there is also some overlap and/or commonality here.

See Brigette Marx, *The Seven Heavenly Courts* (2016); Mike Parsons and Waltraut Reimer have written a diagram titled Heaven's Court System (2017) http://www.freedomtrust.org.uk/website%20stuff/Articles/Court%20system%20of%20heaven%20-%20pt.%201.pdf; Terry Spencer has a Facebook page and a Courts of Heaven area within that and a large group that he moderates that appears to use the same diagram https://www.facebook.com/terryspencer7; and Dr. Ron Horner has written about and named at least 15 heavenly Courts that I could find listed in his writings to date, many of which have identical names to the ones listed above. Dr. Horner calls these collectively the Court System of Heaven. Some of his books which reference these include: *The Courts of Heaven: An Introduction, Engaging the Courts for Your City, Engaging the Courts of Heaven for Ownership & Order, Engaging the Help Desk of the Courts of Heaven, Engaging the Courts of Healing & the Healing Garden, Overcoming Verdicts from the Courts of Hell: Releasing False Judgments, Engaging the Mercy Court of Heaven, Four Keys to Defeating Accusations,* and *Engaging the Courts of Heaven: Maximizing the Power of the Courts of Heaven.*

As a disclaimer, this footnote is provided for informational purposes only, and is not intended as a criticism of any or all of these authors or their ministries in any way. I am not connected with most of them, and, as far as I know, I assume they are all effective ministers, and are helping many people in the body of Christ through their teaching, speaking and writing.

4.  See Psa. 33:5, 37:5-6, 89:14, 97:2, 103:6; Isa. 9:6-7, 16:5, 51:6; Jer. 9:23-24, 22:3; Ezek. 45:9; Amos 5:21-23; Matt. 5:20, 23:23-33.

5.  Strong's Greek, 12. Apparently the demons are both aware and terrified of this place, according to Luke 8:31. See also Rom. 10:7; 2 Pet. 2:4-10; Jude 1:6; Rev. 20:3.

6.  Strong's Greek, 3833.

7.  Strong's Greek, 3528.

8.  Strong's Greek, 3345.

9.  See Rev. 12:7-17.

10.  https://www.rosenfeldinjurylawyers.com/sexual-abuse-lawyer/statute-of-limitations/ and https://simple.wikipedia.org/wiki/Statute_of_limitations.

CHAPTER 4

# PRESENTING, REVIEWING AND WEIGHING THE EVIDENCE IN YOUR CASE

Now that you have given your opening statement, presented a brief summary of your case, and the Judge has issued subpoenas and compelled to appear in this Court the demons assigned to your ancestral bloodline, along with any evidence they possess against you, you are about to see and hear a lot more activity in the Courtroom. In fact, you and/or your prophetic seers should be seeing a large number of demonic spirits in various forms on the Devil's side of the Courtroom now. At least this is typical in most cases, and most ancestral bloodlines. The only exception would be for Defendants who have done an in-depth, extensive amount of prior repentance work for their ancestral bloodlines. They may see fewer demons appear in Court.

At this time, the respective attorneys—Jesus and Satan—are making final preparations for presenting their evidence and calling their witnesses to testify in your case (which will happen after a brief recess). In the meantime, I need to share with you God's view of evidence and proof in heaven's court system. This will lay the groundwork for what is to come next in your case here in this Court.

# GOD RESPECTS AND REQUIRES PROOF AND EVIDENCE

Our God is a God who respects and requires proof and evidence. He demanded proof of Abraham's faith in asking him to sacrifice his only child of promise, Isaac. Once Abraham passed the test, God swore an oath to him in Gen. 22:15-18. He demanded proof of Noah in telling him to build an ark made out of cypress or gopher wood as a sign to a wicked generation. The ark would save Noah and his family, as well as several members of each of the different species of animal life on the earth, in order to preserve a righteous remnant from which to seed or repopulate the earth. Once Noah passed the test, God then made a covenant with Noah and his descendants, and all living creatures on the earth, and offered proof of His covenant to Noah by agreeing to set a rainbow in the clouds as a sign (Gen. 9:8-17).

We see this emphasis on, and requirement of, evidence and proof, reflected both in the Law of Moses and in the New Covenant. Deut. 17:6 (NASB) says:

> On the evidence of two witnesses or three witnesses, he who is to die shall be put to death; he shall not be put to death on the evidence of one witness.

## PRESENTING, REVIEWING AND WEIGHING THE EVIDENCE IN YOUR CASE | 77

Deut. 19:15 (NASB) adds:

> A single witness shall not rise up against a man on account of any iniquity or any sin which he has committed; on the evidence of two or three witnesses a matter shall be confirmed.

Exo. 23:1-2 (ESV, NASB) states:

> You shall not spread a false report. You shall not join hands with a wicked man to be a malicious witness. You shall not follow the masses in doing evil, nor shall you testify in a dispute so as to turn aside after a multitude in order to pervert justice.

Lev. 5:1 (NASB) notes:

> Now if a person sins after he hears a public adjuration to testify when he is a witness, whether he has seen or otherwise known, if he does not tell it, then he will bear his guilt.

Num. 35:30 (ESV, NASB) adds:

> If anyone kills a person, the murderer shall be put to death on the evidence of witnesses. But no person shall be put to death on the testimony of one witness.

Exo. 20:16 (BSB, ESV, NASB, NKJV) writes:

> But you shall not bear false witness against your neighbor.

Prov. 24:28 (ESV) says:

> Be not a witness against your neighbor without cause, and do not deceive with your lips.

It was clearly important to God and His servant Moses that the people of God received due process and a fair hearing in their cases with one another, and with strangers and foreigners, and that the evidence and/or testimony presented by witnesses was relevant and true, respectively, and admissible in a court of law or judicial proceeding. God also provided laws regarding physical evidence.

Exo. 22:10-13 (NIV) states:

> If anyone gives a donkey, an ox, a sheep or any other animal to their neighbor for safekeeping and it dies or is injured or is taken away while no one is looking, the issue between them will be settled by the taking of an oath before the Lord that the neighbor did not lay hands on the other person's property. The owner is to accept this, and no restitution is required. But if the animal was stolen from the neighbor, restitution must be made to the owner. If it was torn to pieces by a wild animal, the neighbor shall bring in the remains as evidence and shall not be required to pay for the torn animal.

Deut. 22: 13-17 (ESV) adds:

> If any man takes a wife and goes in to her and then hates her and accuses her of misconduct and brings a bad name upon her, saying, "I took this woman, and when I came near her, I did not find in her evidence of virginity," then the father of the young woman and her mother shall take and bring out the evidence of her virginity to the elders of the city in the gate. And the father of the young woman shall say to the elders, "I gave my

> *daughter to this man to marry, and he hates her; and behold, he has accused her of misconduct, saying, 'I did not find in your daughter evidence of virginity.' And yet this is the evidence of my daughter's virginity." And they shall spread the cloak before the elders of the city.*

In the New Testament, several proofs or evidence of our adoption into the family of God, and our citizenship in heaven, are mentioned, including: we are a new creation, we have become disciples or followers of Christ, the blood of Christ covers us and speaks on our behalf, our sins have been remitted and forgiven and blotted out by God, we have right standing with God through the righteousness of Christ and our relationship with Him, we are joint heirs with Christ, our names are written in the Lamb's book of life, the Holy Spirit indwells us and helps us as a firstfruits of our inheritance, we have received one or more spiritual gifts, we are doing the works of Jesus, we are persecuted for righteousness' sake, and the oath that God swore to Abraham applies to us today as children of faith, etc.

> WE, AS SAINTS, SHOULD ALSO EXHIBIT A CHANGE IN NATURE AND BEHAVIOR AS WE DEVELOP AND DEMONSTRATE THE FRUITS OF THE SPIRIT.

It follows from these proofs that we, as saints, would also exhibit a change in nature and behavior as we develop and demonstrate the fruits of the Spirit, renew and transform our minds into the mind of Christ, grow and mature into the character of Christ, produce good fruit as we remain connected to Jesus the vine, use our spiritual gifts to serve others, steward well the resources God has given us, make disciples of and from the nations, share the good news of the gospel, work to provide for our needs and families, pray for the needs of others, connect to a local body of believers, read and study the word of God, care for the widows and orphans, etc.

# EYEWITNESS TESTIMONY

The original apostles and Church fathers in the 1st Century A.D. gave eyewitness testimony of Jesus. 2 Pet. 1:16-18 (ESV) says:

> For we did not follow cleverly devised myths when we made known to you the power and coming of our Lord Jesus Christ, but we were eyewitnesses of his majesty. For when he received honor and glory from God the Father, and the voice was borne to him by the Majestic Glory, "This is my beloved Son, with whom I am well pleased," we ourselves heard this very voice borne from heaven, for we were with him on the holy mountain.

1 John 1:1-3 (NIV) adds:

> That which was from the beginning, which we have heard, which we have seen with our eyes, which we have looked at and our hands have touched—this we proclaim concerning the Word of life. The life appeared; we have seen it and testify to it, and we proclaim to you the eternal life, which was with the Father and has appeared to us. We proclaim to you what we have seen and heard, so that you also may have fellowship with us. And our fellowship is with the Father and with his Son, Jesus Christ.

1 Cor. 15:3-8 (NLT) says:

> I passed on to you what was most important and what had also been passed on to me. Christ died for our sins, just as the Scriptures said. He was buried, and he was raised from the dead on the third day, just as the Scriptures said. He was seen by Peter and then by the Twelve. After that, he was seen by more than 500 of his followers at one time, most of whom are still alive, though some have died. Then he was seen by James and later by all the apostles. Last of all, as though I had been born at the wrong time, I also saw him.

John 20:24-29 (NIV) says:

> Now Thomas (also known as Didymus), one of the Twelve, was not with the disciples when Jesus came. So the other disciples told him, "We have seen the Lord!" But he said to them, "Unless I see the nail marks in his hands and put my finger where the nails were, and put my hand into his side, I will not believe." A week later his disciples were in the house again, and Thomas was with them. Though the doors were locked, Jesus came and stood among them and said, "Peace be with you!" Then he said to Thomas, "Put your finger here; see my hands. Reach out your hand and put it into my side. Stop doubting and believe." Thomas said to him, "My Lord and my God!" Then Jesus told him, "Because you have seen me, you have believed; blessed are those who have not seen and yet have believed."

# DUE PROCESS

In addition to physical evidence and eyewitness testimony, Jesus is also interested in due process as a vital and central part of legal and judicial proceedings. John 7:51 (ESV) says:

> "Does our law judge a man without first giving him a hearing and learning what he does?"

The NLT adds:

> "Is it legal to convict a man before he is given a hearing?"

The TPT states:

> He cautioned them, saying, "Does our law decide a man's guilt before we first hear from him and allow him to defend himself?"

The Greek word used for "judge" or "convict" here is *krinei*, from the root *krinó*, meaning: "to judge, decide."[1]

Matt. 18:16 (ESV) says:

> "But if he does not listen, take one or two others along with you, that every charge may be established by the evidence of two or three witnesses."

2 Cor. 13:1 (ESV) notes:

> This is the third time I am coming to you. Every charge must be established by the evidence of two or three witnesses.

I Tim. 5:19 (ESV) states:

PRESENTING, REVIEWING AND WEIGHING THE EVIDENCE IN YOUR CASE | 83

> *Do not admit a charge against an elder except on the evidence of two or three witnesses.*

The Greek word used for "evidence" in both Matt. 18:16 and 2 Cor. 13:1 is *stomatos*, from the root *stoma*, meaning: "the mouth, speech, eloquence in speech, the point of a sword."[2] And the Greek word for "witnesses" here is *martyrōn*, from the root *martus*, meaning: "a witness; an eye- or ear-witness."[3]

Heb. 11:1 (NKJV) says:

> *Now faith is the substance of things hoped for, the evidence of things not seen.*

The Greek word used for "evidence" is *elenchose*, which is from the root *elegchos*, meaning: "a proof, test, persuasion, reproof."[4] Another Greek word translated in Scripture as evidence is *martyrountes*. This is from the root *martureó*, meaning: "to bear witness, testify, give evidence."[5] An example is 1 John 5:7.

1 John 5:4-9 (TPT, author's emphasis) says:

> *You see, every child of God overcomes the world, for our faith is the victorious power that triumphs over the world. So who are the world conquerors, defeating its power? Those who believe that Jesus is the Son of God. Jesus Christ is the One who was revealed as God's Son by his water baptism and by the blood of his cross—not by water only, but by water and blood. And the Spirit, who is truth, confirms this with his testimony. **So we have these three constant witnesses giving their evidence: the Spirit, the water, and the blood. And these three are in agreement.** If we accept the testimony of men, how*

*much more should we accept the more authoritative testimony of God that he has testified concerning his Son?*

The NKJV (author's emphasis) adds:

*For whatever is born of God overcomes the world. And this is the victory that has overcome the world—our faith. Who is he who overcomes the world, but he who believes that Jesus is the Son of God? This is He who came by water and blood—Jesus Christ; not only by water, but by water and blood. And it is the Spirit who bears witness, because the Spirit is truth.* **For there are three that bear witness in heaven: the Father, the Word, and the Holy Spirit; and these three are one. And there are three that bear witness on earth: the Spirit, the water, and the blood; and these three agree as one.** *If we receive the witness of men, the witness of God is greater; for this is the witness of God which He has testified of His Son.*

# THE LAW OF EVIDENCE OR RULES OF EVIDENCE

Now that we have reviewed some of God's laws regarding the use of evidence and testimony in judicial proceedings, in both the Old and New Testament, let's review man's law on this point. According to Wikipedia:

The law of evidence, also known as the rules of evidence, encompasses the rules and legal principles that govern the proof of facts in a legal proceeding. These rules determine what evidence must or must not be considered by the trier of fact in reaching its decision. The trier of fact is a judge in bench trials, or the jury in any cases involving a jury. The law of evidence is also concerned with the quantum (amount), quality, and type of proof needed to prevail in litigation. The rules vary depending upon whether the venue is a criminal court, civil court, or family court, and they vary by jurisdiction.

The quantum of evidence is the amount of evidence needed; the quality of proof is how reliable such evidence should be considered. Important rules that govern admissibility concern hearsay, authentication, relevance, privilege, witnesses, opinions, expert testimony, identification and rules of physical evidence. There are various standards of evidence or standards showing how strong the evidence must be to meet the legal burden of proof in a given situation, ranging from reasonable suspicion to preponderance of the evidence, clear and convincing evidence, or beyond a reasonable doubt.

There are several types of evidence, depending on the form or source. Evidence governs the use of testimony (e.g., oral or written statements, such as an affidavit), exhibits (e.g., physical objects), documentary material, or demonstrative evidence, which are admissible (i.e., allowed to be considered by the trier of fact, such as jury) in a judicial or administrative proceeding (e.g., a court of law).

When a dispute, whether relating to a civil or criminal matter, reaches the court there will always be a number of issues which one party will have to prove in order to persuade the court to find in his or her favor. The law must ensure certain guidelines are set out in order to ensure that evidence presented to the court can be regarded as trustworthy.[6]

Similar to common law legal systems on earth, the burden of proof is on the Plaintiff(s) to prove their charges against the accused, or Defendant(s), in the Courts of Heaven, and Satan and his henchmen must do so beyond a reasonable doubt, and must present clear and convincing evidence to support their charges, and not just a preponderance of evidence. So, Satan and his legal team have their work cut out for them in your case.

You can rest assured that God has rules in place in the Courts of Heaven to ensure that the evidence and testimony introduced and presented, are relevant and admissible, and that both Jesus and Satan are very familiar with these rules. God is an impartial Judge and therefore, His rules of evidence are designed to promote and foster impartiality and fairness. 1 Pet. 1:17 (NKJV) says:

> And if you call on the Father, who without partiality judges according to each one's work, conduct yourselves throughout the time of your stay here in fear.

The NASB adds:

> If you address as Father the One who impartially judges according to each one's work, conduct yourselves in fear during the time of your stay on earth.

Rom. 2:11 (NKJV) says:

> For there is no partiality with God.

Rom. 10:12 (NASB) writes:

> For there is no distinction between Jew and Greek; for the same Lord is Lord of all, abounding in riches for all who call on Him.

Eph. 6:9 (NASB) adds:

*And masters, do the same things to them, and give up threatening, knowing that both their Master and yours is in heaven, and there is no partiality with Him.*

Acts 10:34-35 (NASB) notes:

*Opening his mouth, Peter said: "I most certainly understand now that God is not one to show partiality, but in every nation the man who fears Him and does what is right is welcome to Him."*

This theme is repeated in the Old Testament. Deut. 10:17 (NASB) says:

*For the Lord your God is the God of gods and the Lord of lords, the great, the mighty, and the awesome God who does not show partiality nor take a bribe.*

2 Chron. 19:7 (NASB) adds:

*Now then let the fear of the Lord be upon you; be very careful what you do, for the Lord our God will have no part in unrighteousness or partiality or the taking of a bribe.*

Job 34:18-19 (NIV) states:

*Is he not the One who says to kings, "You are worthless," and to nobles, "You are wicked," who shows no partiality to princes and does not favor the rich over the poor, for they are all the work of his hands?*

Now that I have addressed God's view of the importance of evidence and testimony to due process and impartiality in legal proceedings, and the legal burden of proof that Satan has, let's consider your plea.

It's your spiritual hunger, desperation, and/or curiosity that has brought you here to the Courts of Heaven, rather than a Court summons. That's because appearing in the Courts of Heaven is totally voluntary on your part. God will not force you to do that, and neither will Satan. The Holy Spirit is a gentleman and will not violate your free will. You can suffer unnecessarily from Satan's accusations and demonic influence for as long as you are willing to do so. And, many people endure and tolerate demonic harassment, hindrance, influence, interference, opposition, oppression, or worse, for many years or an entire lifetime! What a needless tragedy that is completely unnecessary.

They do so for a variety of reasons, including fear, ignorance, a sense of powerlessness and/or hopelessness, having accepted a false or compromised identity, not understanding or accepting the authority of the believers in Christ for themselves, suffering from the effects of weak or false teaching in many churches about our victory in Christ or being an overcomer, only knowing about spiritual warfare, and from having a lack of knowledge about the Courts of Heaven.[7] But, thanks be to God, access to the Courts of Heaven is available anytime to the saints as sons and daughters of the Most High God. It's one of the many benefits of the New Covenant. And, there's no time like the present to change your future.

This is obviously a somewhat different process and a different procedural order or sequence than is used in earthly courts, trials and legal systems, and the time and notice elements are highly compressed and greatly accelerated. Such is the realm of the Spirit. If that is hard for you to digest or comprehend, then read

1 Cor. 2:9-16. Accordingly, there is very little need for discovery or depositions, and there are no plea bargains in the Courts of Heaven. Pleas come at the end of the trial, not at the beginning, when the Defendant has learned the charges against them, and has had a chance to repent for these areas of sin in their own life, and in their ancestral bloodline.

# OUR PLEA IS GOD'S MERCY

As saints of God, our plea is all about God's mercy. Jesus has placed His own blood on the mercy seat in heaven, and His blood speaks for us. His blood covers us and His righteousness is imputed to us. Mic. 7:18-19 (NIV) says:

> Who is a God like you, who pardons sin and forgives the transgression of the remnant of his inheritance? You do not stay angry forever but delight to show mercy. You will again have compassion on us; you will tread our sins underfoot and hurl all our iniquities into the depths of the sea.

Rom. 9:15 (BSB, ESV, NASB, NIV, NKJV) adds:

> For He says to Moses, "I will have mercy on whom I have mercy, and I will have compassion on whom I have compassion."

And, Jesus said in Matt. 9:13 (BSB, NIV):

> "But go and learn what this means: 'I desire mercy, not sacrifice.' For I have not come to call the righteous, but sinners."

Mercy is a part of God's nature. Psa. 100:5 (NKJV) notes:

> *For the Lord is good; His mercy is everlasting, And His truth endures to all generations.*

Jas. 2:12-13 (NIV) says:

> *Speak and act as those who are going to be judged by the law that gives freedom, because judgment without mercy will be shown to anyone who has not been merciful. Mercy triumphs over judgment.*

This law is also referred to as the law of liberty in several translations (ESV, KJV, NASB, NKJV) and the law of freedom in others (BSB, CSB, HCS, GW). Heb. 4:16 (NIV) also adds:

> *Let us then approach God's throne of grace with confidence, so that we may receive mercy and find grace to help us in our time of need.*

Jesus also told His disciples the following parable about prayer, and the contrasting heart attitudes and mindsets of two Jewish men, and God's perspective on mercy, in Luke 18:10-14 (NASB):

> *"Two men went up into the temple to pray, one a Pharisee and the other a tax collector. The Pharisee stood and was praying this to himself: 'God, I thank You that I am not like other people: swindlers, unjust, adulterers, or even like this tax collector. I fast twice a week; I pay tithes of all that I get.' But the tax collector, standing some distance away, was even unwilling to lift up his eyes to heaven, but was beating his breast, saying, 'God, be merciful to me, the sinner!' I tell you, this man went to his house justified rather than the*

*other; for everyone who exalts himself will be humbled,*
*but he who humbles himself will be exalted."*

Finally, mercy is a key element and feature of the Parable of the Good Samaritan. Luke 10:25-37 records this story. Jesus told this parable to answer a question from an expert in the law who had asked Jesus, "Who is my neighbor?"

This is a familiar story to most of us about a man who was severely beaten and robbed by bandits while on a short journey from Jerusalem to Jericho, and left for half dead. A Jewish priest passed by him and did nothing to help, as did a Levite. But, a Samaritan had pity for him and took care of him by rendering aid.

At the end of the parable, in verses 36-37, Jesus asked him:

*"Which of these three do you think was a neighbor to*
*the man who fell into the hands of robbers?" The expert*
*in the law replied, "The one who had mercy on him."*
*Jesus told him, "Go and do likewise."*

# COURT PROCEDURE

As is typical in most earthly courts, the Prosecution will present its case first, and opposing counsel (Jesus, your Advocate) will have the opportunity to cross-examine each witness. Then, Jesus will present the Defense's case, and Satan will have the opportunity to cross-examine each witness. Then, each side's attorney will present a closing argument and summary statement, and then rest its case. The Judge will then render a verdict and issue a ruling from the bench.

Just use your sanctified imagination and/or your seer gift, or invite your seers to do so, if any, and sit back and watch the events in the Courtroom unfold before your eyes. Trust your Advocate, Jesus, to defend you as He has unmatched experience in representing God's people, and an unequaled and undefeated track record in Court. So, you are in great hands. Jesus is more than capable and more than competent; He is incomparable and preeminent in His field. He is a legal eagle. Again, stay humble and calm and at peace no matter what you hear or see in the Courtroom, and follow the lead and counsel of your Advocate, Jesus. Don't be insulted or defensive, and don't get offended by Satan's accusations.

Now, let's continue with your case here in the Courts of Heaven. As a reminder, you have given your opening statement, presented a brief summary of your case, and the Judge has issued subpoenas and compelled to appear the demons assigned to your ancestral bloodline, along with any evidence they possess against you. The respective attorneys in your case—Satan and Jesus—are now ready to begin presenting their evidence here in the Courtroom and calling their witnesses to testify. God the Supreme Judge has just ordered your trial to resume, declared the Court back in session, and instructed the respective attorneys to proceed with your case.

It is at this point that you as Defendant(s) will begin to find out what the charges are against you by the Plaintiff(s). These are typically quite serious, and often some of the charges against Defendants in this Court are of a criminal nature and would rise to the level of felonies in an earthly court of law. So, it's to your advantage to address and repent for these sins in your ancestral bloodline as soon as possible. Don't be insulted or defensive, and don't get offended by Satan's accusations. Stay calm and at peace and follow the lead and counsel of your Advocate, Jesus.

Even the original apostles had to learn to deal with their responses until they grew spiritually and matured in their faith. Jesus told Peter in Luke 22:31-34 (NIV, author's emphasis):

> **"Simon, Simon, Satan has asked to sift all of you as wheat. But I have prayed for you, Simon, that your faith may not fail.** And when you have turned back, strengthen your brothers." But he replied, "Lord, I am ready to go with you to prison and to death." Jesus answered, "I tell you, Peter, before the rooster crows today, you will deny three times that you know me."

Satan wants to sift all of the saints, just as he did with Job and the apostles. You are using godly wisdom by not meeting with him first on his turf, on the earth, but instead, meeting with him on God's turf, in the Courts of Heaven, with Jesus at your side.

In the Courtroom, Satan and his henchmen have begun presenting their case against you and introducing evidence and calling their witnesses to testify. Jesus has heard it all before, many times. Typically, my team and I hear a variety of charges against Defendant(s) in a session, originating primarily from their ancestral bloodline, as well as their own sins and the sins of those joined to them by covenant or contract, including idolatry, worship of false gods, involvement with and participation in secret societies, occult and witchcraft, innocent bloodshed, acts of violence, sexual sins, addictions, dysfunctions, lies, curses, financial sins, religious sins, sins of bias/prejudice/discrimination/persecution, and sins of omission. No doubt you and/or your seers, if any, will see and/or hear some of these issues addressed in your case.

Satan and his legal team have now finished presenting their evidence against you and have rested their case. It probably looks bad for you at this point, but it's Jesus' turn to present your defense. After presenting some evidence and calling several witnesses to testify on your behalf, He is now calling you as a final witness in your own defense; and after you are sworn in to testify, you will have ample time to respond to each of Satan's charges by repenting of sins both personally and in your ancestral bloodline, and for those joined to you by covenant. This will take place over an extended period of time as you pray the prayers of repentance in Chapters 6-15, which will become part of the Court record. After you finish praying these prayers of repentance, the evidence against you will all be gone and so will all the demonic spirits which came into the Courtroom to testify against you; such is the power of repentance and mercy. We turn now to Chapter 5, which is the introduction to Part Two, and the prayer templates for the 10 core areas of ancestral bloodline repentance.

## ENDNOTES

1. *Strong's Greek*, 2919.
2. *Strong's Greek*, 4750.
3. *Strong's Greek*, 3144.
4. *Strong's Greek*, 1650.
5. *Strong's Greek*, 3140.
6. Definition is from Wikipedia. https://en.wikipedia.org/wiki/Evidence_(law)
7. See Donald Spellman, *Freedom from Spiritual Bondage*, 2019, Lakebay, WA: Kingdom House Publishing.

PART TWO

# PRAYER TEMPLATES FOR THE 10 CORE AREAS OF ANCESTRAL BLOODLINE REPENTANCE

> "THEREFORE REPENT AND RETURN, SO THAT YOUR SINS MAY BE WIPED AWAY, IN ORDER THAT TIMES OF REFRESHING MAY COME FROM THE PRESENCE OF THE LORD."
>
> – ACTS 3:19 (NASB)

CHAPTER 5
# SETTING THE STAGE FOR REPENTANCE:

## AN INTRODUCTION TO PART TWO

This chapter will briefly introduce the 10 core areas of ancestral bloodline repentance and provide a context and instructions for using the prayer templates. The first nine areas (Chapters 6-14) are sins of commission and the last area (Chapter 15) deals with sins of omission. These are the areas of sin most common to Satanic and demonic influence, interference, accusation, attack, opposition, oppression, harassment, hindrance, schemes, strategies, resistance, and/or torment in all ancestral bloodlines. Your prayers of repentance in these next 10 chapters are all part of your testimony on the witness stand in the Courts of Heaven, since Jesus has called you to testify in your own defense.

The prayer template for each of these 10 areas uses the pronoun "We" as the subject repeatedly and intentionally for maximum effect, breadth and scope. For those not used to or familiar with this style of prayer, it may feel a bit awkward or unnatural initially to pray this way, but after reading one or two prayers you will catch on and pick it up quickly and get used to this approach, and hopefully get comfortable with this style. It gets easier as you go and begin to flow with the Holy Spirit. So, gird up your loins, take courage, and step out in faith as you pray.

The prayer templates are written in the plural "we" because they follow the style of the identificational repentance prayers prayed by Nehemiah and Daniel for the Jewish people and the Jewish nation. Neh. 1:1-11 is a model prayer in this regard, especially verses 6-7 (NIV), which read:

> "[L]et your ear be attentive and your eyes open to hear the prayer your servant is praying before you day and night for your servants, the people of Israel. I confess the sins we Israelites, including myself and my father's family, have committed against you. We have acted very wickedly toward you. We have not obeyed the commands, decrees and laws you gave your servant Moses."

Verse 11 (NIV) is also enlightening:

> "Lord, let your ear be attentive to the prayer of this your servant and to the prayer of your servants who delight in revering your name. Give your servant success today by granting him favor in the presence of this man."

As we know from biblical history, these prayers were extremely effective and powerful and produced amazing, tremendous results.

Similarly, Daniel prayed for his people in Dan. 9:1-27. In particular, verses 4-19 (NIV) contain the prayer of Daniel. It was such a moving and powerful prayer of confession and repentance of sins for the Jews, that the messenger angel Gabriel was sent to Daniel immediately and arrived while Daniel was still *"speaking and praying, confessing my sin and the sin of my people Israel and making my request to the Lord my God for his holy hill—while I was still in prayer, Gabriel, the man I had seen in the earlier vision, came to me in swift flight about the time of the evening sacrifice."* This prayer moved heaven to action. Your prayers in the Courts of Heaven can and should do the same if they are sincere and from the heart.

# USING THE PRAYER TEMPLATES

So, in the prayer templates which follow in this section, the word "We" represents and stands for all three of the following groups: yourself, your ancestral bloodline, and all of those who are joined to you by covenant or contract. This is the essence of identificational repentance, which is to pray for your sins and the sins of your people or people group (ethnos), which can be a single nation or tribe, or can encompass several nations or tribes.[1]

The ancestral bloodline is a microcosm and subset of this larger people group, and the phrase "those who are joined to us by covenant" includes all those who have joined our extended family in ways other than blood relations, such as adoption, marriage, business contracts, fraternal organizations or secret societies in which oaths, vows, pledges, covenants, or curses are spoken and/or solemnized. You can also pray identificational repentance prayers for individuals in a wide range of contexts and settings.[2]

The nine chapters dealing with sins of commission include Idolatry, False Gods, Freemasonry and Secret Societies, Occult and Witchcraft, Sexual Sins, Innocent Bloodshed and Acts of Violence, Financial Sins and Mammon, Addictions, Dysfunctions, Religion, and Racial/Gender/Age and Cultural Bias/Prejudice/ Discrimination and Persecution. Then, there is one last chapter with a prayer of repentance for sins of omission to deal with anything still left in the ancestral bloodline that has not been dealt with or covered earlier. 1 Pet. 4:8 (CSB, ESV, HCS, NASB, NLT) says that *"love covers a multitude of sins."* In like manner, so does heartfelt, sincere repentance mixed with grace.

The approach and goal for each of the prayer templates for these next 10 chapters is to systematically and comprehensively help saints to address and resolve or settle legally the outstanding root issues in their ancestral bloodline for each of these areas of sin, through identificational repentance from a representative (you) of their ancestral bloodline who has legal standing in the Courts of Heaven. This is a wholistic and forensic approach rather than a single issue approach, since the prayers that follow in the next 10 chapters, address and encompass every possible area of sin common to all bloodlines. There is a small amount of overlapping of terms in the prayers, since several of the issues being prayed for could easily fit within more than one area of sin.

THESE PRAYERS HAVE BEEN EFFECTIVE AND FRUITFUL FOR A LARGE NUMBER OF PEOPLE.

These are each Spirit-breathed and Spirit-led prayers which were downloaded to me by the Holy Spirit, and that my team and I use with people all over the world on a regular basis as we minister in the Courts of Heaven. We have seen these prayers be effective and fruitful for a large number of people globally in a wide variety and range of cultural and personal settings and circumstances, by helping to bring them increased relief, freedom, and breakthrough—sometimes incrementally and quietly, and sometimes exponentially and dramatically. The amount of relief, freedom, and breakthrough received and/or experienced, varies from person to person because there are so many variables or factors involved in each case.

For each of the prayer templates, feel free to add other items that the Holy Spirit quickens to you or brings to your remembrance or awareness or sanctified imagination. No one set of written prayers should ever be viewed as a silver bullet that will solve all problems and address all issues, but these will help you to resolve all past sins in your life and in your ancestral bloodline. And, I can say these prayers have been field tested and refined and expanded on a continuing basis over a seven-year period with excellent results from a large number of people in 25-30 nations.

## LET THE HOLY SPIRIT LEAD YOU THROUGH

We also need the help of the Holy Spirit, who will lead and guide us into all truth as we follow His leading and prompting. God may have previously revealed or shown you in a dream or vision, or through the gentle whisper or nudge of the Holy Spirit, an outstanding issue of sin in your life or your ancestral bloodline, that needs repentance. That is always helpful and a good place to start. However, most people do find it very useful and quite helpful to have a prayer template to use as a guide for each of the 10 core areas of sin, as it provides a starting place or jumping off point in prayer that you can build on and add to as needed. I encourage you to use both—the prayer templates as a baseline, and then add your own spontaneous prayers from the heart for emphasis, reinforcement and impact.

Listen to the Holy Spirit as you pray and read these prayer templates and add anything else that He tells you or brings to your mind or quickens to your spirit. Don't be in a rush as you read the prayer templates out loud. There is power in the spoken word, so we advise and encourage Defendants to read these prayers out loud rather than silently to themselves. There are several important reasons for and benefits in doing this.

First, my team and I record the sessions we lead in the Courts of Heaven via Zoom. That way, we are able to provide Defendants with a link to their recording after the session for their own personal reflection and use and future access, and so that they have a link to this recording to remind them of what happened during their session and to be able to refer back to this time whenever they want to. Likewise, you can also record your own session, and I recommend that you do that.

Second, you are here in the Courts of Heaven as a Defendant, and are reading the prayers of repentance for the 10 core areas of sin in your ancestral bloodline. Since this becomes part of the Court record for your case, it is important that the Judge, the Court reporter, your legal team, Satan and his henchmen and demonic horde, all hear you state these prayers verbally and, preferably, forcefully, with some gusto. However, if you have a pronounced speech impediment or have a deaf mute condition, are deaf or have significant hearing loss or some other condition, then God will know and understand that, and you can just pray silently. He won't expect or require you to do anything you're not physically or mentally capable of doing.

If there is more than one Defendant in a session, then you can either pray the prayers which follow in later chapters in unison, or one at a time, as you prefer. Sometimes it can be helpful to repeat a certain phrase or portion of a prayer more than once if the Holy Spirit quickens that to you or seems to be hovering there. And, occasionally you may feel led to read one of the prayers that stands out to you or touches you in a deep way, a second time for emphasis. If you have prophetic seers with you in your session, they can help guide you. Above all, be led by the Spirit.

In the Courts of Heaven, different spiritual beings are gathered and assembled together, as recorded in Hebrews 12 and many other Scriptures. A record is being kept of the Courtroom proceedings in heaven. The Judge hears testimony and views evidence. As well, the enemy gets to hear your prayers of repentance and watch the effect that has in real time on his evidence against you through your ancestral bloodline. Jesus is also there as your Advocate. You have the Holy Spirit living inside of you to help you and, as mentioned earlier, we frequently encounter many holy angels and some members of the great Cloud of Witnesses in the Courts of Heaven.

Finally, as we near the end of this chapter and you prepare to begin addressing the first core area in prayer in the next chapter, I want to briefly mention the importance and advantage of having one or more prophetic seers with you in your Courts of Heaven session(s). Actually, that is one of many reasons that I have written this book. Obviously, not everyone in the body of Christ is a seer; therefore, many believers are challenged or limited in their ability to access the Courts of Heaven due to not being seers or knowing seers or having access to seers, or having the faith or understanding to step into the reality and practical application of Eph. 2:5-6 and Psa. 24:3-6 on either a one-time or more frequent basis.

These prayer templates have been written and shared with you and made available to the body of Christ so that every born-again, blood-bought disciple and follower of Christ can have access to the Courts of Heaven—whether or not you are a seer—and can have available a protocol, prayer strategy and a set of prayer templates to use for approaching and entering the Courts of Heaven. These will help you in presenting your case, reviewing the evidence against you, repenting of any unconfessed or unresolved sins in your ancestral bloodline, entering a plea, resting your case, and then receiving a verdict from the Judge.

This can all be done with or without having seers as part of your session, although having seers can be helpful. Some people are seers and can handle that role themselves, although it is usually more effective to have other seers present. Others may know one or more seers, or can access them through their local church or denomination, or a multitude of recognized and respected prophetic ministries, or the list of Hub Leaders posted on Robert Henderson's website https://gpec.world/global-reformer-hubs.

Having one or more seers as part of your session is like having sports broadcasters, color commentators and play analysts present at a football game. Obviously, the teams, players, referees, officials and fans who have season passes and the league sanctioning the sport can all have the game played without the broadcasters, commentators and analysts present. But, they are helpful and beneficial because they add insight, understanding, history, context, and commentary for the millions of fans watching or listening remotely to sports events and games by telecast, live streaming, podcast or radio.

However, since you, as a representative of your ancestral bloodline with legal standing, are doing the real work of identificational repentance for your bloodline through your prayers, it is possible to present your case in the Courts of Heaven without having one or more seers present. After all, John 10:2-5, 14-16 says we can each hear and understand and obey the voice of the Good Shepherd, Jesus. As children of God and saints of the Most High, we have the Holy Spirit living inside of us, and according to 1 Cor. 2:9-16 and Rom. 8:26-27, we are designed and hardwired for Spirit to spirit communication. Thus, we are each designed to hear God directly and personally. Your spiritual hearing can also be increased through use and practice and by stirring up the gifts within you, according to Heb. 5:14 and 2 Tim. 1:6-7.

This book will help to make the heavenly dimension more accessible to many believers around the world so that they, too, can present their cases in the Courts of Heaven, repent for their ancestral bloodlines through prayer, and obtain a verdict from the just, holy and impartial Supreme Judge. And, for those who have no understanding of or experience with, and no grid or context for modern day seers (prophets),[3] then take heart, because this book is written for you. It will guide you through a set of prayer templates which include identificational repentance to help you address sins in your ancestral bloodline in the Courts of Heaven and to help you find

THIS BOOK IS WRITTEN FOR YOU.

and experience increased relief, freedom and breakthrough in your life and family. Now we turn our attention to Chapter 6.

AUTHOR'S NOTE:

Please be aware that the last sentence (boldfaced) of the Occult and Witchcraft Prayer template on page 139 in Chapter 8 deals with closing and sealing demonic portals and gateways. This sentence can be prayed with any of the other prayer templates for other areas of sin on an as needed basis if you, Holy Spirit or your seers discern there are open demonic portals and/or gateways that need to be closed elsewhere as well.

## ENDNOTES

1. See Dennis Wiedrick, *A Royal Priesthood: Reigning with Christ through Intercession*, 1997, 2016, Calgary, AB, Canada: Wiedrick and Associates, Apostolic Ministries.
2. Ibid.
3. See Dr. Bruce Cook, *Partnering with the Prophetic: Portfolios, Protocols, Patterns & Processes* (3rd Ed.), 2011, 2014, Lakebay, WA: Kingdom House Publishing.

# CHAPTER 6
# IDOLATRY AND FALSE GODS

Idolatry means the practice of worshipping, exalting, deifying and/or serving false gods. In a formal sense, this refers to false deities. Idolatry is prevalent and common in many parts of the world, and I have seen idols and temples built to honor and worship false gods in the nations where I have traveled and ministered. For example, Hinduism alone in India has some three million gods and goddesses. Such cultures practice polytheism, which means the belief in and worship of more than one god. This is in contrast to nations which practice monotheism, which means the doctrine or belief that there is only one God. Most nations and empires throughout history have been polytheistic, including the Akkadian Empire, Assyrian Empire, Babylonian Empire, Egyptian Empire, Macedonian Greek Empire, Roman Empire, Persian Empire, etc., according to Wikipedia.

In the Old Testament era, a few of the false gods worshipped in the Middle Eastern region surrounding Israel included Baal,

Ashtoreth, Asherah, Ashur, Dagon, Marduk, Molech, and the Queen of Heaven. Others included Ahura Mazda, Atar, Haoma, Vayu, Zorvan, Tiri, Tishtrya, Verethragna, Mithra, Rashnu, Angra Mainyu, Hvar Ksata, Ardvi Sura Anahita, An, Enlil, Enki, Hadad, Ishtar, Sin, and Shamash, according to Wikipedia. In the Book of Acts, the seat of worship of the Greek goddess Artemis also known as the Roman goddess Diana, was the temple in Ephesus, capital of the Roman province of Asia. Ancient Greece was polytheistic according to Paul the Apostle, who debated the Greek philosophers in a meeting of the Areopagus in Athens. Acts 17:16 (NIV) says:

> While Paul was waiting for them in Athens, he was greatly distressed to see that the city was full of idols.

In a broader, less formal sense, idols are whatever you give undue priority and a place of honor, preeminence, and adoration to, and communion with, in the place of God. This can include objects, substances, other people, your spouse, children, work, or even ministry. Idols are, in a practical sense, anything you value above God or put in the place of God. Even emotional or psychological pain can become an idol, as can nature, sports, pleasure, recreation, entertainment, and self-gratification.

As recorded in Exo. 20:3-6 (NIV), the first two of the 10 Commandments in the Law of Moses are as follows:

> "You shall have no other gods before Me. You shall not make for yourself an idol in the form of anything in heaven above or on the earth beneath or in the waters below. You shall not bow down to them or worship them; for I, the Lord your God, am a jealous God, punishing the

*children for the sin of the fathers to the third and fourth generation of those who hate me, but showing love to a thousand generations of those who love me and keep my commandments."*

God knew that the human heart can be fickle. That's why He made these two commandments first among the 10 Commandments He gave to Moses and the Jewish people. Jer. 17:9-10 (NIV) says:

*The heart is deceitful above all things and beyond cure. Who can understand it? "I, the Lord search the heart and examine the mind, to reward each person according to their conduct, according to what their deeds deserve."*

The NKJV goes even further and describes the human heart as "desperately wicked."

*The heart is deceitful above all things, And desperately wicked; Who can know it? "I, the Lord, search the heart, I test the mind, Even to give every man according to his ways, according to the fruit of his doings."*

The hearts of God's people were repeatedly stubborn and rebellious in the Old Testament, beginning with them making a golden calf in the wilderness as an idol and then worshipping it while Moses was on top of Mount Sinai meeting with God for 40 days. Then later, they refused to believe the report of Joshua and Caleb, and died in the wilderness because of their fear and unbelief. It was their children and grandchildren who entered the Promise Land 40 years later, along with Joshua and Caleb. Jer. 2:5b (NIV) says:

*"They followed worthless idols and became worthless themselves."*

A common theme among Old Testament prophets for the Jewish people was repentance and returning or turning back to God, and the consequences of not doing so. Mic. 2:13-15 (NLT) states:

*"I will destroy all your idols and sacred pillars, so you will never again worship the work of your own hands. I will abolish your idol shrines with their Asherah poles and destroy your pagan cities. I will pour out my vengeance on all the nations that refuse to obey me."*

Many translations (NIV, BSB, NASB, CSB, HCS) say in verse 15:

*"I will take vengeance in anger and wrath on the nations that have not obeyed Me."*

Gideon first had to pass a test before he could be trusted by God with an army and a nation. Judg. 6:25-27 (NIV) says:

*That same night the Lord said to him, "Take the second bull from your father's herd, the one seven years old. Tear down your father's altar to Baal and cut down the Asherah pole beside it. Then build a proper kind of altar to the Lord your God on the top of this height. Using the wood of the Asherah pole that you cut down, offer the second bull as a burnt offering."*

*So, Gideon took ten of his servants and did as the Lord told him. But, because he was afraid of his family and the townspeople, he did it at night rather than in the daytime.*

You and I likewise are called to destroy false altars today in prayer, and to set in place and/or raise up godly altars.

God asked the nation of Israel a rhetorical question through the prophet Isaiah. Isa. 40:18-20 (ESV) says:

> To whom then will you liken God, or what likeness compare with him? An idol! A craftsman casts it, and a goldsmith overlays it with gold and casts for it silver chains. He who is too impoverished for an offering chooses wood that will not rot; he seeks out a skillful craftsman to set up an idol that will not move.

Verse 25 asks again:

> "To whom will you compare me? Or who is my equal?" says the Holy One.

Then, God challenges the nations of the earth and their gods to display the same power and wisdom as Israel's God in Isa. 41:1 (NIV, author's emphasis):

> "Be silent before me, you islands! Let the nations renew their strength! **Let them come forward and speak; let us meet together at the place of judgment.**"

Where else would that place be but in front of the throne of God in the Courts of Heaven? Then, in verses 21-24 (NIV) of that same chapter, God takes the nations and their idols to Court, questions them, and passes judgment on them.

> "Present your case," says the Lord. "Set forth your arguments," says Jacob's King. "Tell us, you idols, what is going to happen. Tell us what the former things were, so that we may consider them and know their final outcome. Or declare to us the things to come, tell us what the future holds, so we may know that you are

*gods. Do something, whether good or bad, so that we will be dismayed and filled with fear. But you are less than nothing and your works are utterly worthless; whoever chooses you is detestable."*

God's verdict and judgment is that idols are "less than nothing" and their works are "utterly worthless," and whatever nation or individual chooses to worship an idol is "detestable." In fact, God views idolatry as spiritual adultery (Jer. 3:1-2, 6, 9, 13, 5:7, 9:2).

Finally, Isaiah 59 is a fascinating and vivid picture of God's view of a nation in need of repentance (Israel) because of their idolatry and wickedness. The entire nation needed a Courts of Heaven session. Verses 1-15 (NIV) say:

*Surely the arm of the Lord is not too short to save, nor his ear too dull to hear. But your iniquities have separated you from your God; your sins have hidden his face from you, so that he will not hear. For your hands are stained with blood, your fingers with guilt. Your lips have spoken falsely, and your tongue mutters wicked things. No one calls for justice; no one pleads a case with integrity. They rely on empty arguments, they utter lies; they conceive trouble and give birth to evil.*

*They hatch the eggs of vipers and spin a spider's web. Whoever eats their eggs will die, and when one is broken, an adder is hatched. Their cobwebs are useless for clothing; they cannot cover themselves with what they make. Their deeds are evil deeds, and acts of violence are in their hands. Their feet rush into sin; they are swift to shed innocent blood. They pursue evil schemes; acts of violence mark their ways. The way of peace they do not know; there is no justice in their paths. They have turned them into crooked roads; no one who walks along them will know peace.*

*So justice is far from us, and righteousness does not reach us. We look for light, but all is darkness; for brightness, but we walk in deep shadows. Like the blind we grope along the wall, feeling our way like people without eyes. At midday we stumble as if it were twilight; among the strong, we are like the dead. We all growl like bears; we moan mournfully like doves. We look for justice, but find none; for deliverance, but it is far away.*

*For our offenses are many in your sight, and our sins testify against us. Our offenses are ever with us, and we acknowledge our iniquities: rebellion and treachery against the Lord, turning our backs on our God, inciting revolt and oppression, uttering lies our hearts have conceived. So justice is driven back, and righteousness stands at a distance; truth has stumbled in the streets, honesty cannot enter. Truth is nowhere to be found, and whoever shuns evil becomes a prey. The Lord looked and was displeased that there was no justice.*

This description could be equally applicable today to some nations. This is a tragic and sobering picture of a nation in desperate need of corporate repentance and a return to God.

Notice that verse 12 says, "*our sins testify against us.*" This testimony would have been given in the Courts of Heaven.

Many centuries later, Jesus reiterated the importance of putting God first in our lives when He said in Matt. 6:33 (NKJV):

> "*But seek first the kingdom of God and His righteousness, and all these things shall be added to you.*"

When asked which is the greatest commandment in the law, in Matt. 22:35-40 (BSB, NIV), Jesus answered:

> "'*Love the Lord your God with all your heart and with all your soul and with all your mind.' This is the first and greatest commandment. And the second is like it: 'Love your neighbor as yourself.' All the Law and the Prophets hang on these two commandments.*"

Luke 10:27 (ESV, NASB) gives a similar account:

> *And He answered, "You shall love the Lord your God with all your heart, and with all your soul, and with all your strength, and with all your mind; and your neighbor as yourself.*"

With this in mind, you can begin reading aloud the prayer of repentance below now. Please remember that you are testifying as a witness under oath in your own defense in the Courts of Heaven, and this and other prayers which follow in subsequent chapters will become part of the Court record. I invite you to pray this powerful prayer of repentance now.

# REPENT FOR ROOT ISSUES/SINS OF IDOLATRY/FALSE GODS AND CLEANSE ANCESTRAL BLOODLINE

## PRAYER TEMPLATE

We renounce and repent of, and cut ties to and break agreement with, all idolatry and worship of false gods, including but not limited to: ancestral worship; worship of or agreement with or sacrifice to false gods, demonic spirits, Satan, Lucifer, and the Devil; worshipping at evil altars; demonic ceremonies and/or rituals at altars, in temples, or other places; worshipping the dead; worshipping objects, substances and/or people instead of or more than God; worshipping nature, the sun, moon, stars and/or constellations instead of or more than God; worshipping money, ambition, work, sex, pain, grief, heartache, bitterness, disappointment, and/or unforgiveness instead of or more than God; worshipping self-will, dreams, desires or ego instead of or more than God.

IN JESUS NAME, AMEN! And we forgive all those connected to us by bloodline, covenant and/or contract who have practiced or participated in these things.

Feel free to add anything else to this prayer that the Holy Spirit brings to your mind or spirit in this area of Idolatry and False Gods. Take as long as you need to deal with this area thoroughly in your ancestral bloodline. When you are finished, turn to the next chapter.

# PRAYER SESSION NOTES

## CHAPTER 7
# FREEMASONRY AND SECRET SOCIETIES

One definition of a secret society is "an organization whose members are sworn to secrecy about its activities." Wikipedia defines it as "a club or an organization whose activities, events, inner functioning, or membership are concealed from non-members. The society may or may not attempt to conceal its existence." Secret societies are anathema to the Christian faith. They invariably involve secret oaths, vows, rituals, rites, and rules. Some organizations, such as the Order of Freemasonry, even include curses at each level or degree of Masonry. We are children of the light, and secrets usually involve darkness.

These curses are not just for the initiate, but for his family, and are often generational in nature, and are evil and quite violent and punitive. They are meant to act as a strong deterrent to either dropping out or resigning from membership, or divulging lodge secrets and violating his oaths and/or vows. Family members of

Masons seem to be prone or susceptible to health issues such as asthma, emphysema, cystic fibrosis, heart disease, diabetes, blood pressure disorders, cancer, and others that are related to the curses used by the organization, both as a requirement of membership, and for promotion or advancement to higher degrees within Freemasonry or the Masonic.

Oath is defined as "a solemn promise, often invoking a divine witness, regarding one's future action or behavior." Vow is defined as "a solemn promise, or a set of promises, committing oneself to a prescribed role, calling, or course of action." Vows are often used for weddings when two people are joined together in marriage, and also for those entering the priesthood or a monastic or religious order. When someone is elected to public office, often there is a "swearing in" ceremony where they take the oath of office for a role or position of public service. Oaths are also used for induction into military service and the armed forces, and for those testifying in a trial or legal proceeding in a court of law or before a grand jury.

Matt. 5:33-37 (NIV) says:

> "Again, you have heard that it was said to the people long ago, 'Do not break your oath, but fulfill to the Lord the vows you have made.' But I tell you, do not swear an oath at all: either by heaven, for it is God's throne; or by the earth, for it is his footstool; or by Jerusalem, for it is the city of the Great King. And do not swear by your head, for you cannot make even one hair white or black. All you need to say is simply 'Yes' or 'No'; anything beyond this comes from the evil one."

The NLT says:

> "You have also heard that our ancestors were told, 'You must not break your vows; you must carry out the vows you make to the Lord.' But I say, do not make any vows! Do not say, 'By heaven!' because heaven is God's throne. And do not say, 'By the earth!' because the earth is his footstool. And do not say, 'By Jerusalem!' for Jerusalem is the city of the great King. Do not even say, 'By my head!' for you can't turn one hair white or black. Just say a simple, 'Yes, I will,' or 'No, I won't.' Anything beyond this is from the evil one."

The NKJV says:

> "Again you have heard that it was said to those of old, 'You shall not swear falsely, but shall perform your oaths to the Lord.' But I say to you, do not swear at all: neither by heaven, for it is God's throne; nor by the earth, for it is His footstool; nor by Jerusalem, for it is the city of the great King. Nor shall you swear by your head, because you cannot make one hair white or black. But let your 'Yes' be 'Yes,' and your 'No,' 'No.' For whatever is more than these is from the evil one."

I believe the intent and context of what Jesus is saying here in this passage is not that we cannot participate in wedding vows or religious vows or oaths of public office, induction into military service, and/or testifying in a trial or legal proceeding in a court of law or before a grand jury, all of which are part of life. Instead, we should use extreme caution and be very careful and vigilant and prayerful about the vows and oaths that we do make, since these can give Satan a legal right to accuse us if or when we break them. God takes covenants seriously, and so should we. Covenants are a life and death matter.

One example of a violent vow is found in Gen. 4:23-24 (NIV): Lamech said to his wives:

> "Adah and Zillah, listen to me; wives of Lamech, hear my words. I have killed a man for wounding me, a young man for injuring me. If Cain is avenged seven times, then Lamech seventy-seven times."

This is a bloodthirsty boast. The NLT adds:

> One day Lamech said to his wives, "Adah and Zillah, hear my voice; listen to me, you wives of Lamech. I have killed a man who attacked me, a young man who wounded me. If someone who kills Cain is punished seven times, then the one who kills me will be punished seventy-seven times!"

Lamech was moving in the opposite spirit of Christ, who told Peter in Matt. 18:21-22 to forgive someone who offends you not just seven times, but up to seventy times seven (also translated as 77 times).

Another example of a foolish and rash vow is mentioned in Judges 11:29-39 (NLT):

> At that time the Spirit of the Lord came upon Jephthah, and he went throughout the land of Gilead and Manasseh, including Mizpah in Gilead, and from there he led an army against the Ammonites. And Jephthah made a vow to the Lord. He said, "If you give me victory

*over the Ammonites, I will give to the Lord whatever comes out of my house to meet me when I return in triumph. I will sacrifice it as a burnt offering."*

*So Jephthah led his army against the Ammonites, and the Lord gave him victory. He crushed the Ammonites, devastating about twenty towns from Aroer to an area near Minnith and as far away as Abel-keramim. In this way Israel defeated the Ammonites.*

*When Jephthah returned home to Mizpah, his daughter came out to meet him, playing on a tambourine and dancing for joy. She was his one and only child; he had no other sons or daughters. When he saw her, he tore his clothes in anguish. "Oh, my daughter!" he cried out. "You have completely destroyed me! You've brought disaster on me! For I have made a vow to the Lord, and I cannot take it back."*

*And she said, "Father, if you have made a vow to the Lord, you must do to me what you have vowed, for the Lord has given you a great victory over your enemies, the Ammonites. But first let me do this one thing: Let me go up and roam in the hills and weep with my friends for two months, because I will die a virgin."*

*"You may go," Jephthah said. And he sent her away for two months. She and her friends went into the hills and wept because she would never have children. When she returned home, her father kept the vow he had made, and she died a virgin.*

I also want to share a few other Scriptures that are helpful in understanding vows, oaths and curses. Prov. 26:2 (NKJV) says, "*Like a flitting sparrow, like a flying swallow, So a curse without cause shall not alight.*" This is helpful sometimes when emotions or misunderstandings are involved and someone curses you recklessly or in the heat of the moment without merit or without thinking things through. Unfortunately, in many cases, Satan has a legal right through the ancestral bloodline to accuse and attack you and perpetuate a generational curse. A member of the bloodline with standing in heaven, has to stand in the gap and repent for the underlying sins and curses in order to remove or resolve that in the Courts of Heaven. One example of this is when Joshua cursed the City of Jericho after capturing, conquering and destroying it. Josh. 6:26 says (NIV):

> *At that time Joshua pronounced this solemn oath: "Cursed before the LORD is the one who undertakes to rebuild this city, Jericho: At the cost of his firstborn son he will lay its foundations; at the cost of his youngest he will set up its gates."*

The NLT adds:

> *At that time Joshua invoked this curse: "May the curse of the LORD fall on anyone who tries to rebuild the town of Jericho. At the cost of his firstborn son, he will lay its foundation. At the cost of his youngest son, he will set up its gates."*

The Good News Translation (GNT) states:

> *At this time Joshua issued a solemn warning: "Anyone who tries to rebuild the city of Jericho will be under*

*the LORD's curse. Whoever lays the foundation will lose his oldest son; Whoever builds the gates will lose his youngest."*

And the HCS notes:

*At that time Joshua imposed this curse: "The man who undertakes the rebuilding of this city, Jericho, is cursed before the LORD. He will lay its foundation at the cost of his firstborn; he will set up its gates at the cost of his youngest."*

So, whether this curse was from Joshua, or from the Lord, or both, the curse was serious enough and had enough authority behind it that it was still in effect over 600 years and 15 to 20 generations later.[1] 1 Kings 16:34 (NIV) says:

*In Ahab's time, Hiel of Bethel rebuilt Jericho. He laid its foundations at the cost of his firstborn son Abiram, and he set up its gates at the cost of his youngest son Segub, in accordance with the word of the Lord spoken by Joshua son of Nun.*

This Scripture illustrates the point that generational curses can span hundreds of years and many generations, and still be potent and in effect.

Curses are serious things and not to be taken lightly. Many people have curses that remain active in their ancestral bloodlines, that they have no idea about. My team and I see this on a regular basis as we minister to and with other people in the Courts of Heaven. We often see the curses in scroll form on the evidence table in the Courtroom. As repentance is made by

Defendant(s) for areas of sin in their ancestral bloodline, we see the scroll(s) containing curses burned up in real time in heaven on the evidence table. This is often a very dramatic and climactic moment for Defendant(s).

Another biblical example is found in Acts 23:12-15 (NIV):

> *The Jews bound themselves to an oath they swore to kill Paul. The next morning some Jews formed a conspiracy and bound themselves with an oath not to eat or drink until they had killed Paul. More than forty men were involved in this plot. They went to the chief priests and the elders and said, "We have taken a solemn oath not to eat anything until we have killed Paul. Now then, you and the Sanhedrin petition the commander to bring him before you on the pretext of wanting more accurate information about his case. We are ready to kill him before he gets here."*

The MSG adds (author's emphasis):

> *Next day the Jews worked up a plot against Paul. They took a solemn oath that they would neither eat nor drink until they had killed him. **Over forty of them ritually bound themselves to this murder pact and presented themselves to the high priests and religious leaders.** "We've bound ourselves by a solemn oath to eat nothing until we have killed Paul. But we need your help. Send a request from the council to the captain to bring Paul back so that you can investigate the charges in more detail. We'll do the rest. Before he gets anywhere near you, we'll have killed him. You won't be involved."*

Since it was not yet Paul's appointed time to die, and God had other work and plans for him to accomplish and fulfill, this plot was discovered or found out by Paul's nephew, reported to the commander of the Roman garrison in Jerusalem, and foiled or thwarted. The commander ordered two centurions to muster and assemble a force of 470 Roman soldiers to escort Paul and transport him that same night under heavy armed guard and cover of darkness to Antipatris, 30 miles distant, and the next morning on to Caesarea, the headquarters of Roman rule for Samaria and Judea, which was 28 miles further. The commander also wrote an official letter and sent that with his troops, and entrusted Paul to the care of Antonius Felix, Governor of Judea, at Herod's Palace.

Other examples of vows and curses are found in Deut. 28:15-24, Ruth 1:1-4:22, Josh. 8:31-35, and Rev. 22:18-19. Ruth contains a famous vow that many couples like to incorporate in their wedding vows. Ruth 1:16-17 (NIV) says:

> But Ruth replied, "Don't urge me to leave you or to turn back from you. Where you go I will go, and where you stay I will stay. Your people will be my people and your God my God. Where you die I will die, and there I will be buried. May the Lord deal with me, be it ever so severely, if even death separates you and me."

Because of the covenant nature of God with Israel and the Jewish people, and the covenants God made and the oaths He swore with Abraham, Isaac and Jacob, He and His human leaders Moses and Joshua, in successive generations, would present the many favorable and delightful blessings of the covenant first, for those who obeyed God, followed by the equally numerous and unfavorable and unpleasant curses of the covenant, for those who chose to disobey God.

Deut. 28:15-24 (NLT) records this farewell warning from Moses:

> "But if you refuse to listen to the Lord your God and do not obey all the commands and decrees I am giving you today, all these curses will come and overwhelm you: Your towns and your fields will be cursed. Your fruit baskets and breadboards will be cursed. Your children and your crops will be cursed. The offspring of your herds and flocks will be cursed. Wherever you go and whatever you do, you will be cursed.

> "The Lord himself will send on you curses, confusion, and frustration in everything you do, until at last you are completely destroyed for doing evil and abandoning Me. The Lord will afflict you with diseases until none of you are left in the land you are about to enter and occupy. The Lord will strike you with wasting diseases, fever, and inflammation, with scorching heat and drought, and with blight and mildew. These disasters will pursue you until you die. The skies above will be as unyielding as bronze, and the earth beneath will be as hard as iron. The Lord will change the rain that falls on your land into powder, and dust will pour down from the sky until you are destroyed."

The NKJV adds this:

> "But it shall come to pass, if you do not obey the voice of the Lord your God, to observe carefully all His

*commandments and His statutes which I command you today, that all these curses will come upon you and overtake you: Cursed shall you be in the city, and cursed shall you be in the country. Cursed shall be your basket and your kneading bowl. Cursed shall be the fruit of your body and the produce of your land, the increase of your cattle and the offspring of your flocks. Cursed shall you be when you come in, and cursed shall you be when you go out. The Lord will send on you cursing, confusion, and rebuke in all that you set your hand to do, until you are destroyed and until you perish quickly, because of the wickedness of your doings in which you have forsaken Me.*

*"The Lord will make the plague cling to you until He has consumed you from the land which you are going to possess. The Lord will strike you with consumption, with fever, with inflammation, with severe burning fever, with the sword, with scorching, and with mildew; they shall pursue you until you perish. And your heavens which are over your head shall be bronze, and the earth which is under you shall be iron. The Lord will change the rain of your land to powder and dust; from the heaven it shall come down on you until you are destroyed."*

Josh. 8:31-35 (NKJV) says:

*Now Joshua built an altar to the Lord God of Israel in Mount Ebal, as Moses the servant of the Lord had commanded the children of Israel, as it is written in the Book of the Law of Moses: "an altar of whole stones over which no man has wielded an iron tool." And they offered on it burnt offerings to the Lord, and sacrificed peace offerings. And there, in the presence of the children of Israel, he wrote on the stones a copy of the law of Moses, which he had written.*

*Then all Israel, with their elders and officers and judges, stood on either side of the ark before the priests, the Levites, who bore the ark of the covenant of the Lord, the stranger as well as he who was born among them. Half of them were in front of Mount Gerizim and half of them in front of Mount Ebal, as Moses the servant of the Lord had commanded before, that they should bless the people of Israel. And afterward he read all the words of the law, the blessings and the cursings, according to all that is written in the Book of the Law. There was not a word of all that Moses had commanded which Joshua did not read before all the assembly of Israel, with the women, the little ones, and the strangers who were living among them.*

Josh. 8:31-35 (NIV) says:

*Then Joshua built on Mount Ebal an altar to the Lord, the God of Israel, as Moses the servant of the Lord had commanded the Israelites. He built it according to what is written in the Book of the Law of Moses—an altar of uncut stones, on which no iron tool had been used. On it they offered to the Lord burnt offerings and sacrificed fellowship offerings. There, in the presence of the Israelites, Joshua wrote on stones a copy of the law of Moses.*

> All the Israelites, with their elders, officials and judges, were standing on both sides of the ark of the covenant of the Lord, facing the Levitical priests who carried it. Both the foreigners living among them and the native-born were there. Half of the people stood in front of Mount Gerizim and half of them in front of Mount Ebal, as Moses the servant of the Lord had formerly commanded when he gave instructions to bless the people of Israel. Afterward, Joshua read all the words of the law—the blessings and the curses—just as it is written in the Book of the Law. There was not a word of all that Moses had commanded that Joshua did not read to the whole assembly of Israel, including the women and children, and the foreigners who lived among them.

Rev. 22:18-19 (NIV) says:

> I warn everyone who hears the words of the prophecy of this scroll: If anyone adds anything to them, God will add to that person the plagues described in this scroll. And if anyone takes words away from this scroll of prophecy, God will take away from that person any share in the tree of life and in the Holy City, which are described in this scroll.

Rev. 22:18-19 (NLT) adds:

> And I solemnly declare to everyone who hears the words of prophecy written in this book: If anyone adds anything to what is written here, God will add to that person the plagues described in this book. And if anyone removes any of the words from this book of prophecy, God will

*remove that person's share in the tree of life and in the holy city that are described in this book.*

This concludes our discussion of curses, vows and oaths.

With this in mind, you can begin reading aloud the prayer of repentance below now. Please remember that you are testifying as a witness under oath in your own defense in the Courts of Heaven, and this and other prayers which follow in subsequent chapters will become part of the Court record. I invite you to pray this powerful prayer of repentance now.

## ENDNOTE

1. Six hundred (600) years would be 15 generations using 40 years per generation, and 20 generations using 30 years per generation.

# REPENT FOR ROOT ISSUES/ SINS OF FREEMASONRY/SECRET SOCIETIES AND CLEANSE ANCESTRAL BLOODLINE

## PRAYER TEMPLATE

We renounce and repent of, and cut ties to and break agreement with, all secret societies, and their attendant and associated oaths, vows, curses, covenants, rites, rituals, rules, acts and activities, including but not limited to Freemasonry, including both the Scottish rite branch with 33 degrees, and the York rite branch with 10 degrees, and their sister organization for women, the Eastern Star; DeMolay; Rainbow Girls; Rastafarianism; Rosicrucianism; Luciferianism; the One World Order; the Order of the Illuminati; the Club of Rome; the Bilderbergers; La Cosa Nostra (Mafia); the Communist Party; the Nazi Party (National Socialist German Workers' Party); Hitler Youth; Neo-Nazi groups; the Ku Klux Klan; racial supremacy groups; gangs; and other private, fraternal organizations, clubs, and societies to which we may have joined, belonged to, been a member of, sworn allegiance to, been initiated by, or paid dues to. We renounce and repent of, and cut ties to and break agreement with, any and all unholy alliances, plots, plans, schemes, vows, oaths, curses, conspiracies, covenants, and worship of or agreement with false gods, evil spirits, Satan, Lucifer, the Devil, Beelzebub or Baphomet, and we cancel, retract, nullify and declare void any human creeds, vows, oaths, curses, covenants and/or initiation rites and rituals that we signed or agreed to or swore an oath to or participated in or with, or were connected to in any way, that violate the Bible (Word of God/Holy Scriptures), or that endangered, jeopardized, harmed and/or cursed innocent lives, ancestral family members, assets, animals or livestock, property or possessions.

IN JESUS NAME, AMEN!

And we forgive all those connected to us by bloodline, covenant and/or contract who have practiced or participated in these things.

Feel free to add anything else to this prayer that the Holy Spirit brings to your mind or spirit in this area of Freemasonry and Secret Societies. Take as long as you need to deal with this area thoroughly in your ancestral bloodline. When you are finished, turn to the next chapter.

# PRAYER SESSION NOTES

# CHAPTER 8
# OCCULT AND WITCHCRAFT

Almost all bloodlines have some history with or exposure to the occult and witchcraft. These range in severity and intensity from childhood or juvenile exposure to tarot cards, Ouija boards, horoscopes, psychics, mediums, and online role-playing games involving the occult, to blood covenants with the powers of darkness, being treated for illness by a shaman, generational curses from witches or warlocks or wizards, animal sacrifices, human sacrifices, spells and incantations, and Satanic Ritual Abuse (SRA). This is one of the worst of the areas because of its inherent evil, rebellion, violence, anti-Christ spirit, hatred of God and His people, and worship of and allegiance to Satan.

Here are a few examples from Scripture that reveal God's attitude toward and view of the occult and witchcraft. Mic. 5:12 (NIV) says:

> "I will destroy your witchcraft and you will no longer cast spells."

Luke 10:18 records (NKJV):

*And He [Jesus] said to them, "I saw Satan fall like lightning from heaven."*

Satan, the father of witchcraft, was rather unceremoniously kicked out of heaven by God for his pride, ambition, overinflated ego, and rebellion, among other things. He was the original Absalom spirit before Absalom was even born (see 2 Sam. 15:1-6). Rev. 12:3-9 tells us that along with Satan came a third of the angels, who had joined him in the rebellion and were defeated in their war against God and the holy angels. These fallen angels are also called demons or demonic spirits.

As I mentioned in Chapter 1, Satan's kingdom is built on darkness, deception, lies, and counterfeits. He tries to copy God's kingdom, but his futile attempts are pitiful and doomed to ultimate failure. Witches, warlocks, shamans, soothsayers, sorcerers, enchanters, magicians, and the like form Satan's priesthood. Several pagan, secular rulers in the Old Testament had astrologers, enchanters, magicians, and sorcerers at the royal court. Included were Pharaoh, in Egypt, who had Moses and Aaron to contend with, and Nebuchadnezzar, in Babylon, who had Daniel, Shadrach, Meshach, and Abednego to serve him and provide wise counsel and dream interpretation. Pharaoh and his army were no match for the power of God, and Daniel rose to prominence in Babylon as the royal advisor and chief *satrap* (governor or administrator).

OCCULT AND WITCHCRAFT | 135

A notable example from the Old Testament is the witch of Endor, whom King Saul came to visit on the day before his death. 1 Sam. 28:7-25 (NLT) reads:

> Saul then said to his advisors, "Find a woman who is a medium, so I can go and ask her what to do." His advisers replied, "There is a medium at Endor."
>
> So Saul disguised himself by wearing ordinary clothing instead of his royal robes. Then he went to the woman's home at night, accompanied by two of his men. "I have to talk to a man who has died," he said. "Will you call up his spirit for me?" "Are you trying to get me killed?" the woman demanded. "You know that Saul has outlawed all the mediums and all who consult the spirits of the dead. Why are you setting a trap for me?" But Saul took an oath in the name of the Lord and promised, "As surely as the Lord lives, nothing bad will happen to you for doing this."
>
> Finally, the woman said, "Well, whose spirit do you want me to call up?" "Call up Samuel," Saul replied. When the woman saw Samuel, she screamed, "You've deceived me! You are Saul!" "Don't be afraid!" the king told her. "What do you see?" "I see a god coming up out of the earth," she said. "What does he look like?" Saul asked. "He is an old man wrapped in a robe," she replied. Saul realized it was Samuel, and he fell to the ground before him. "Why have you disturbed me by calling me back?" Samuel asked Saul.

"Because I am in deep trouble," Saul replied. "The Philistines are at war with me, and God has left me and won't reply by prophets or dreams. So I have called for you to tell me what to do." But Samuel replied, "Why ask me, since the Lord has left you and has become your enemy? The Lord has done just as he said he would. He has torn the kingdom from you and given it to your rival, David. The Lord has done this to you today because you refused to carry out his fierce anger against the Amalekites. What's more, the Lord will hand you and the army of Israel over to the Philistines tomorrow, and you and your sons will be here with me. The Lord will bring down the entire army of Israel in defeat."

Saul fell full length on the ground, paralyzed with fright because of Samuel's words. He was also faint with hunger, for he had eaten nothing all day and all night. When the woman saw how distraught he was, she said, "Sir, I obeyed your command at the risk of my life. Now do what I say, and let me give you a little something to eat so you can regain your strength for the trip back." But Saul refused to eat anything. Then his advisers joined the woman in urging him to eat, so he finally yielded and got up from the ground and sat on the couch. The woman had been fattening a calf, so she hurried out and killed it. She took some flour, kneaded it into dough and baked unleavened bread. She brought the meal to Saul and his advisers, and they ate it. Then they went out into the night.

Saul and his three sons died the next day in battle against the Philistines on the slopes of Mount Gilboa overlooking the Jezreel Valley. Is it any wonder that God made it a capital offense in the Old Testament to consult with a medium or a witch? (See for example Exo. 22:18; Lev. 20:27; and 1 Chron. 10:13.)

My team and I have observed, while participating in numerous Courts of Heaven sessions, that this area seems to be one of two areas that most directly affect a saint's ability and/or capacity to see and hear in the Spirit, with the other area being Religion. We have noticed that once someone has prayed the prayer of repentance which follows, that often there is a removal of a demonic blockage or hindrance, and a release of the ability and/ or an increase in the capacity, to see and hear in the Spirit, or both. This can also happen after praying the prayer of repentance for the Religion area or the Addictions area, but we see it more often after the Occult/Witchcraft area has been dealt with in the ancestral bloodline.

With this in mind, you can begin reading the prayer of repentance which follows. Please remember that you are testifying as a witness under oath in your own defense in the Courts of Heaven, and this and other prayers which follow in subsequent chapters will become part of the Court record. I invite you to pray this powerful prayer of repentance now.

# REPENT FOR ROOT ISSUES/SINS OF OCCULT/WITCHCRAFT AND CLEANSE ANCESTRAL BLOODLINE

## PRAYER TEMPLATE

We renounce and repent of, and cut ties to and break agreement with, all occult acts and activities, oaths and covenants, including but not limited to: magic, voodoo, Santeria, spells and incantations, hexes and vexes, lotions and potions, sorcery, soothsaying, psychics, mediums, séances, palm reading, fortune telling, tarot cards, 8 ball, Ouija boards, astral projection, telekinesis, spirit guides, horoscopes, astrology, water witching, role-playing computer or online games such as Dungeons & Dragons® and Diablo® and Pokémon® and World of Warcraft®, the Harry Potter series of books and movies, horror movies, amulets, charms, talismans, superstitions, curses, evil altars, blood sacrifices, demonic ceremonies and/or rituals at temples or evil altars, secret oaths, secret rituals, divination, necromancy, shamanism, reading tea leaves, insubordination, rebellion, worship of false gods, worship of nature, worship of celestial bodies – the sun and moon and stars and constellations, worship of water spirits, worship of ancestral beings or deities, worship of Satan, blood covenants, idolatry, paganism, hedonism, licentiousness, debauchery, orgies, self-mutilation, poltergeists (ghosts), Satanic ritual abuse (SRA), Spiritual Response Therapy (SRT), DaSilva Method, Kaballah, Reiki, ESP, Eckankar, New Age, yoga, Kundalini, chanting, Spiritism, hypnotism, channeling,

OCCULT AND WITCHCRAFT | 139

levitation, table topping, mind programming, mind reading, mind control, and phrenology, as well as every act of renouncing or cursing God, Jesus, Holy Spirit, heaven or hell. **We ask you Lord to close and seal any demonic portals or gateways that are open in my life, in my ancestral bloodline or in those joined to us by covenant or contract.**

IN JESUS NAME, AMEN! And we forgive all those connected to us by bloodline, covenant and/or contract who have practiced or participated in these things.

Feel free to add anything else to this prayer that the Holy Spirit brings to your mind or spirit in this area of the Occult and Witchcraft. Take as long as you need to deal with this area thoroughly in your ancestral bloodline. When you are finished, turn to the next chapter.

# PRAYER SESSION NOTES

140 | PRAYERS FOR CLEANSING ANCESTRAL BLOODLINES IN THE COURTS OF HEAVEN

## CHAPTER 9
# SEXUAL SINS

Human sexuality is a beautiful gift, but like other gifts, it must be stewarded wisely and used within proper boundaries to be healthy and holy, and to be pleasing to God. Sexual intercourse and intimacy in God's plan is reserved exclusively for a husband and wife in the sacred covenant of marriage, or holy matrimony. There is a leaving and a cleaving involved, and a threefold cord between the couple and God. Gen. 2:24 (BSB) says:

> *For this reason a man will leave his father and mother and be united to his wife, and they will become one flesh.*

The NASB and NKJV say, *"joined to his wife."* Matt. 19:4-5 repeats this Scripture, then verse 6 (NIV) says:

> *Therefore what God has joined together, let no one separate.*

Heb. 13:4 (BSB) says:

*Marriage should be honored by all and the marriage bed kept undefiled, for God will judge the sexually immoral and adulterers.*

The marriage covenant is a covenant of honor, love, trust, respect, communication and holiness or purity. This is illustrated and demonstrated both in the Song of Songs in the epic, poetic love story between King Solomon and the Shulammite woman, and also in Paul's writings about how husbands and wives should treat one another in Eph. 5:22-33 as well as 1 Cor. 7:1-7.

Eph. 5:1-5 (BSB, NIV, author's emphasis) states:

*Be imitators of God, therefore, as dearly loved children and live a life of love, just as Christ loved us and gave himself up for us as a fragrant offering and sacrifice to God. **But among you there must not be even a hint of sexual immorality, or of any kind of impurity, or of greed,** because these are improper for God's holy people ... For of this you can be sure: No immoral, impure or greedy person—such a man is an idolater—has any inheritance in the kingdom of Christ and of God.*

Sexual immorality is also listed as a sin worthy of death that will be judged by God. Rev. 21:8 (NIV) says:

*But the cowardly, the unbelieving, the vile, the murderers, the sexually immoral, those who practice magic arts, the idolaters and all liars—they will be consigned to the fiery lake of burning sulfur. This is the second death.*

SEXUAL SINS | 143

1 Cor. 6:12-20 (NIV, author's emphasis) states:

> "I have the right to do anything," you say—but not everything is beneficial. "I have the right to do anything"—but I will not be mastered by anything. You say, "Food for the stomach and the stomach for food, and God will destroy them both." **The body, however, is not meant for sexual immorality but for the Lord, and the Lord for the body.** By his power God raised the Lord from the dead, and he will raise us also. Do you not know that your bodies are members of Christ himself? Shall I then take the members of Christ and unite them with a prostitute? Never! Do you not know that he who unites himself with a prostitute is one with her in body? For it is said, "The two will become one flesh." **But whoever is united with the Lord is one with him in spirit.**
>
> Flee from sexual immorality. **All other sins a person commits are outside the body, but whoever sins sexually, sins against their own body. Do you not know that your bodies are temples of the Holy Spirit,** who is in you, whom you have received from God? You are not your own; you were bought at a price. Therefore **honor God with your bodies.**

Paul said in 1 Cor. 7:1-5 (BSB):

> Now for the matters you wrote about: It is good to abstain from sexual relations. But because there is so much sexual immorality, each man should have his own wife, and each woman her own husband. The husband

*should fulfill his marital duty to his wife, and likewise the wife to her husband. The wife does not have authority over her own body, but the husband. Likewise the husband does not have authority over his own body, but the wife. Do not deprive each other, except by mutual consent and for a time, so you may devote yourselves to prayer. Then come together again, so that Satan will not tempt you through your lack of self-control.*

Paul then gives instruction in 1 Cor. 7:8-9 (BSB) to those who are single and to widows (and by extension, widowers):

*Now to the unmarried and widows I say this: It is good for them to remain unmarried, as I am. But if they cannot control themselves, let them marry. For it is better to marry than to burn with passion.*

The desire of most people to have a mate—and for many, a godly mate—has resulted in a plethora of Internet dating sites, executive dating services, matchmakers, matchmaking services, and television shows about dating and courtship. Even so, Holy Spirit is still the best matchmaker in history and in the universe— just listen to His still, small voice.

We have a promise from our Heavenly Father in Psa. 68:5-6 (NLT):

*Father to the fatherless, defender of widows—this is God, whose dwelling is holy. God places the lonely in families; he sets the prisoners free and gives them joy. But he makes the rebellious live in a sun-scorched land.*

The NKJV states:

*A father of the fatherless, a defender of widows, is God in His holy habitation. God sets the solitary in families; He brings out those who are bound into prosperity; But the rebellious dwell in a dry land.*

The MSG adds:

*Father of orphans, champion of widows, is God in his holy house. God makes homes for the homeless, leads prisoners to freedom, but leaves rebels to rot in hell.*

The Passion Translation (TPT) writes:

*To the fatherless he is a father. To the widow he is a champion friend. To the lonely he makes them part of a family. To the prisoners he leads into prosperity until they sing for joy. This is our Holy God in his Holy Place! But for the rebels there is heartache and despair.*

Finally, Solomon, the wisest man who ever lived, wrote in Prov. 6:26-35 (NLT):

*For a prostitute will bring you to poverty, but sleeping with another man's wife will cost you your life. Can a man scoop a flame into his lap and not have his clothes catch on fire? Can he walk on hot coals and not blister his feet? So it is with the man who sleeps with another man's wife. He who embraces her will not go unpunished. Excuses might be found for a thief who steals because he is starving. But if he is caught, he must pay back seven times what he stole, even if he has to sell everything in his house.*

*But the man who commits adultery is an utter fool, for he destroys himself. He will be wounded and disgraced. His shame will never be erased. For the woman's jealous husband will be furious, and he will show no mercy when he takes revenge. He will accept no compensation, nor be satisfied with a payoff of any size.*

# BREAKING SOUL TIES

I recommend that while you are repenting of sexual sins, you break soul ties with any and all former lovers, including ex-spouses (if any), with whom you engaged in sex outside of marriage. You can pray this simple prayer, "Lord Jesus, I repent and break soul ties with all former lovers with whom I engaged in sex outside of the covenant of marriage. I send back to him/her/them everything that belongs to him/her/them from our relationship without harm, and I take back to myself, everything that belongs to me from our relationship without harm. And I sever these soul ties now, in Jesus' mighty name!" Obviously, you should not break a soul tie with your current marriage partner, boyfriend or girlfriend. With these things in mind, you can begin reading the prayer of repentance that follows. Please remember that you are testifying as a witness under oath in your own defense in the Courts of Heaven, and this and other prayers which follow in subsequent chapters will become part of the Court record. I invite you to pray this powerful prayer of repentance now.

# REPENT FOR ROOT ISSUES OF SEXUAL SINS AND CLEANSE ANCESTRAL BLOODLINE

## PRAYER TEMPLATE

We renounce and repent of, and cut ties to and break agreement with, all sexual sins, including but not limited to: lust, infatuation, emotional affairs, fornication, adultery, rape, incest, sexual molestation, inappropriate touching or kissing, sex trafficking, sexual abuse, sexual grooming, pedophilia, prostitution, pornography, orgies, sexual perversion, homosexuality, bisexuality, sodomy, bestiality, masturbation, fetishes, exhibitionism, voyeurism, dressing inappropriately or immodestly, cross dressing, transgender, gender conversion, conversion therapy, inappropriate flirtation, inappropriate seduction, sexual addiction, sexual rituals, sexual domination, inappropriate sexual thoughts, viewing individuals as sexual objects, unholy or impure sexual acts, sexual contamination (movies, music), lechery, lewdness, lasciviousness, treating sex as less than holy and pure in marriage, withholding sex and/or intimacy and/or affection in marriage, trading sex for favors or power, using sex for control in a relationship, having sex with demons or spiritual spouse, emotional unavailability in marriage, being a stripper, call girl, hooker, escort, gigolo, madam, masseuse, mistress, sugar baby, sugar daddy, whore, whoremonger, pimp, pedophile, or sexual predator.

IN JESUS NAME, AMEN! And we forgive all those connected to us by bloodline, covenant and/or contract who have practiced or participated in these things.

Feel free to add anything else to this prayer that the Holy Spirit brings to your mind or spirit in this area of Sexual Sins. Take as long as you need to deal with this area thoroughly in your ancestral bloodline. When you are finished, turn to the next chapter.

## PRAYER SESSION NOTES

CHAPTER 10
# INNOCENT BLOODSHED AND ACTS OF VIOLENCE

Perhaps one of the vilest areas to deal with in your ancestral bloodline, is this one. While each of these areas is evil and despicable, this one is especially perverse, heinous, and horrific, since it involves such issues as murder, suicide, abortion, euthanasia, martyrdom, rape, incest, terrorism, slavery, human trafficking, sex trafficking, gang activity, torture, and abuse of all types, among others. These are crimes for the most part perpetrated against the most innocent and vulnerable among us—the unborn still in their mother's womb, children, teenagers, civilians, women and the elderly. And, in many nations of the world, Christians and church leaders—especially pastors—are targeted for their faith by oppressive government regimes, as well as radical religious zealots of other faiths, including Muslims and Hindus.

Unfortunately, despite the more than 400 years that have passed since the Dutch West Indies Company was chartered in 1621 and the Portuguese began slave trading in 1526, and the 1400 years since the Arabs began slave trading in the 7th Century,[1] the misery and horror and inhumanity of human and sex trafficking is still with us. Of course, slavery originated much earlier in antiquity with the earliest civilizations, and victorious nations in war routinely subjugated the conquered peoples and took some of them captive as slaves. Joseph's brothers sold him into slavery for 20 shekels of silver to Midianite merchants in Genesis 37, who in turn sold Joseph into slavery to Potiphar, Pharaoh's captain of the guard. And, the first recorded murder was by one brother against another in a premeditated act of jealous anger. This, of course, is the story of Cain and Abel, the first two offspring or progeny of Adam and Eve, recorded in Genesis 4.

Their story is instructive for us, as it relates to ancestral bloodline repentance, and so we will look at it briefly. Gen. 4:2-12 (NIV, author's emphasis) says:

> Now Abel kept flocks, and Cain worked the soil. In the course of time Cain brought some of the fruits of the soil as an offering to the Lord. And Abel also brought an offering—fat portions from some of the firstborn of his flock. The Lord looked with favor on Abel and his offering, but on Cain and his offering he did not look with favor. So Cain was very angry, and his face was downcast.
>
> Then the Lord said to Cain, "Why are you angry? Why is your face downcast? **If you do what is right, will you not be accepted? But if you do not do what is right, sin is**

> *crouching at your door; it desires to have you, but you must rule over it."* Now Cain said to his brother Abel, *"Let's go out to the field." While they were in the field, Cain attacked his brother Abel and killed him. Then the Lord said to Cain, "Where is your brother Abel?""I don't know," he replied. "Am I my brother's keeper?"*

> *The Lord said, "What have you done? Listen!* **Your brother's blood cries out to me from the ground. Now you are under a curse and driven from the ground, which opened its mouth to receive your brother's blood from your hand.** *When you work the ground, it will no longer yield its crops for you. You will be a restless wanderer on the earth."*

First of all, each brother brought an offering to the Lord, but Cain's offering was not acceptable or not pleasing to the Lord, while his brother Abel's offering was looked upon favorably by the Lord. Cain reacted to God's displeasure by becoming angry and downcast. Then, his flesh rose up and took control of him. He gave in to his feelings and emotions, and probably the angry thoughts his mind generated.

Even though God cared enough to seek out Cain and give him some loving correction and a strong warning, Cain ignored and rejected God's counsel and warning, and took out his frustration, shame, depression, and anger on Abel, and plotted to deceive and murder him. After Cain carried out his devilish plan, and killed his brother, Cain then compounded his sin by lying to God about what he had done. This resulted in a curse being placed on Cain by God, and he became a restless wanderer in the earth.

We see here in this story many of the issues and elements that are listed below in the prayer of repentance. The process that Cain and many others throughout history have gone through, is described in Jas. 1:13-15 (NIV):

> When tempted, no one should say, "God is tempting me." For God cannot be tempted by evil, nor does he tempt anyone; but each person is tempted when they are dragged away by their own evil desire and enticed. Then, after desire has conceived, it gives birth to sin; and sin, when it is full-grown, gives birth to death.

Rom. 6:23 (BSB, CSB, NIV, NKJV) adds:

> For the wages of sin is death, but the gift of God is eternal life in Christ Jesus our Lord.

The choice is very clear, and each person gets to make it. With this in mind, you can begin reading the prayer of repentance now. Please remember that you are testifying as a witness under oath in your own defense in the Courts of Heaven, and this and other prayers which follow in subsequent chapters will become part of the Court record. I invite you to pray this powerful prayer of repentance now.

## ENDNOTE

1. https://en.m.wikipedia.org/wiki/History_of_slavery. Also, see https://brycchancarey.com/slavery/chrono4.htm.

# REPENT FOR ROOT ISSUES/SINS OF INNOCENT BLOODSHED/ ACTS OF VIOLENCE AND CLEANSE ANCESTRAL BLOODLINE

## PRAYER TEMPLATE

We renounce and repent of, and cut ties to and break agreement with, all innocent bloodshed and acts of violence, including but not limited to: abortion, unlawful executions, assassinations, murders, genocide, ethnic cleansing, mercenaries, euthanasia, untimely or premature death, suicide, cannibalism, sedition, treason, slander, libel, false accusations, false judgments, gossip, lies, character assassination, dishonor, disrespect, betrayal, backbiting, backstabbing, deception, subterfuge, political intrigue, political spirit, espionage, conspiracy, intimidation, assault, bullying, threats, sabotage, martyrdom, persecution, beatings, torture, brutality, cruelty, inhumanity, mutilation, rape, incest, molestation, stealing innocence, unholy vows or oaths, unholy covenants, acts of terrorism, insurrection, mutiny, rioting, vigilantism, gang initiations, gang activity, slavery, sex trafficking, human trafficking, kidnapping, trespassing, arson, poaching, mayhem, vandalism, graffiti, coercion, and abuse of all types—spiritual, mental, verbal, physical, sexual, emotional, psychological and religious abuse.

IN JESUS NAME, AMEN! And we forgive all those connected to us by bloodline, covenant and/or contract who have practiced or participated in these things.

Feel free to add anything else to this prayer that the Holy Spirit brings to your mind or spirit in this area of Innocent Bloodshed and Acts of Violence. Take as long as you need to deal with this area thoroughly in your ancestral bloodline. When you are finished, turn to the next chapter.

# PRAYER SESSION NOTES

## CHAPTER 11
# FINANCIAL SINS AND MAMMON

The area of money, riches, wealth, assets and possessions is another big one in terms of the potential for sin in ancestral bloodlines. Eccl. 5:10 (NIV) says:

> Whoever loves money never has enough; whoever loves wealth is never satisfied with their income.

Matt. 6:24 (NKJV) states:

> "No one can serve two masters, for either he will hate the one and love the other, or else he will be loyal to one and despise the other. You cannot serve both God and Mammon."

This is so true! Our hearts and our loyalty cannot be divided. We must intentionally, purposely and covenantally choose God as our master, weighing the cost in advance.

Luke 16:10-11 (KJV, NKJV) adds:

*"He that is faithful in that which is least is faithful also in much: And he that is unjust in the least is unjust also in much. If therefore you have not been faithful in the unrighteous Mammon, who will commit to your trust the true riches?"*

1 Tim. 6:9-10 (NASB) notes:

*But those who want to get rich fall into temptation and a snare and many foolish and harmful desires which plunge men into ruin and destruction. For the love of money is a root of all kinds of evil.*

Heb. 13:5 (NIV) says:

*Keep your lives free from the love of money and be content with what you have, because God has said, "Never will I leave you, never will I forsake you."*

The words "temptation" and "snare" and "desires" in this last verse in Greek are, respectively, *peirasmon, pagida* and *epithymias.* **Temptation** is from the root word *peirasmos* and means: "an experiment, a trial, temptation, calamity, affliction." **Snare** is from the root word *pagis*, which means: "trap, snare, stratagem, device, wile." **Desires** is from the root word *epithumia*, which means: "desire, passionate longing, lust."[1] And, notice these are "foolish and harmful desires," i.e., carnal and fleshly desires. This is similar language to that found in Jas. 1:13-15, which we cited in an earlier chapter.

Literally, since money and Mammon are translated from the same Greek word *mamōna*, they are used interchangeably in most Scriptures, and have a seducing allure or appeal similar to sexual desire or lust. Thus, money can be addicting or seducing like sex and drugs. If you don't master it, it will master you, and it can be a cruel master (*kurios* in Greek, meaning lord). Mammon is from the root word *mamónas*, which means "riches, money, possessions, property."[2]

**IF YOU DON'T MASTER MONEY, IT WILL MASTER YOU.**

The roots of Mammon include greed, corruption (graft/bribes/kickbacks/extortion/blackmail), denying people justice or permits, lust, seduction, envy, idolatry (worship/service), deception, betrayal/lies (violating our word, breaking contracts and covenants), fraud/theft/stealing/embezzlement (Ponzi schemes, tax evasion, bank robbery), entitlement (welfare), control (wanting to monopolize trade or pricing or supply). The oil and gas (energy) cartels and Federal Reserve are examples of this latter point. Satan has a heyday with these, and many Christians fall prey to one or more of these demonic roots. The results are often devastating and disastrous, and can include poverty, bankruptcy, imprisonment, divorce, damaged reputation, and/or premature death.

In contrast, God's plan is that we prosper and be in abundance as we worship, serve, honor and trust Him, in order to fulfill His covenant with our spiritual ancestors Abraham, Isaac and Jacob, and bless us. Deut. 8:18 (NIV) says:

> But remember the Lord your God, for it is he who gives you the ability to produce wealth, and so confirms his covenant, which he swore to your ancestors, as it is today.

The NLT adds:

*Remember the Lord your God. He is the one who gives you power to be successful, in order to fulfill the covenant he confirmed to your ancestors with an oath.*

And the MSG states,

*Remember that God, your God, gave you the strength to produce all this wealth so as to confirm the covenant that he promised to your ancestors—as it is today.*

The Hebrew word for "work" and "worship" is the same word, *avodah*, which says a lot about how God sees the role and function of work in our lives. Money is just a tool and should not be our first or highest priority. That belongs to God alone, exclusively. Matt. 6:31-33 (NKJV) states:

*"Therefore do not worry, saying, 'What shall we eat?' or 'What shall we drink?' or 'What shall we wear?' For after all these things the Gentiles seek. For your heavenly Father knows that you need all these things. But seek first the kingdom of God and His righteousness, and all these things shall be added to you."*

The NLT adds:

*"So don't worry about these things, saying, 'What will we eat? What will we drink? What will we wear?' These things dominate the thoughts of unbelievers, but your heavenly Father already knows all your needs. Seek the Kingdom of God above all else, and live righteously, and he will give you everything you need."*

Verse 33 in the TPT says:

*"So above all, constantly chase after the realm of God's kingdom and the righteousness that proceeds from him. Then all these less important things will be given to you abundantly."*

Matt. 6:21 (BSB, CSB, ESV, HCS, NASB, NIV, NKJV) says:

*"For where your treasure is, there your heart will be also."*

God has shown us His heart by sharing His greatest treasure with us and sowing the seed of His own Son as a sacrifice and ransom for all mankind. Rom. 8:32 (NIV) says:

*He who did not spare his own Son, but gave him up for us all—how will he not also, along with him, graciously give us all things?*

The TPT says:

*For God has proved his love by giving us his greatest treasure, the gift of his Son. And since God freely offered him up as the sacrifice for us all, he certainly won't withhold from us anything else he has to give.*

The MSG adds:

*If God didn't hesitate to put everything on the line for us, embracing our condition and exposing himself to the worst by sending his own Son, is there anything else he wouldn't gladly and freely do for us?*

Our trust and security should be in God and not in chariots, horses, armies, riches or money, which can be fleeting, ephemeral, short-lived, transitory and temporary. Jas. 4:13-14 (NASB) says:

> *Come now, you who say, "Today or tomorrow we will go to such and such a city, and spend a year there and engage in business and make a profit." Yet you do not know what your life will be like tomorrow. You are just a vapor that appears for a little while and then vanishes away.*

God and His kingdom are recession- and depression-proof and unshakeable, and He is able to meet our needs and then some.

Phil. 4:19 (BSB) states:

> *And my God will supply all your needs according to His glorious riches in Christ Jesus.*

2 Cor. 9:8-10 (NIV) adds:

> *And God is able to bless you abundantly, so that in all things at all times, having all that you need, you will abound in every good work. As it is written: "They have freely scattered their gifts to the poor; their righteousness endures forever." Now he who supplies seed to the sower and bread for food will also supply and increase your store of seed and will enlarge the harvest of your righteousness.*

It pays to serve God. David said in Psa. 37:25 (NKJV):

> *I have been young, and now am old; Yet I have not seen the righteous forsaken, Nor his descendants begging bread.*

God knows how to take care of His own.

There are three main types of gifts and giving mentioned in Scripture: alms for the poor, including widows and orphans (benevolence), tithes, and offerings. The righteous participate in all three, not just tithes. Matt. 6:19 (NASB) says:

> *"Do not store up for yourselves treasures on earth, where moth and rust destroy, and where thieves break in and steal. But store up for yourselves treasures in heaven, where neither moth nor rust destroys, and where thieves do not break in or steal."*

We are able to do this by giving into God's work on the earth for those in need of physical and spiritual resources. This encompasses a wide range of organizations including His ministers and ministries, parachurch ministries, NGOs, and charities of all types.

With this in mind, you can now begin reading the prayer of repentance below. Please remember that you are testifying as a witness under oath in your own defense in the Courts of Heaven, and this and other prayers which follow in subsequent chapters will become part of the Court record. I invite you to pray this powerful prayer of repentance now.

# REPENT FOR ROOT ISSUES OF FINANCIAL SINS/MAMMON AND CLEANSE ANCESTRAL BLOODLINE

## PRAYER TEMPLATE

We renounce and repent of, and cut ties to and break agreement with, all financial sins, including but not limited to: theft, fraud, robbery, stealing, bribes, kickbacks, deception, dishonest gain, dishonest and unethical business practices, not honoring contracts, kidnapping, ransom, extortion, poverty, lack, entitlement, excessive debt, blackmail, piracy, compulsion, unjust weights and measures, double sets of books or false entries, embezzlement, blood money, greed, hoarding, corruption, seduction of money, loan sharking, usury, unjustly annexing or transferring title to property or assets of others, not giving to the poor, not giving offerings, withholding tithes, or giving less than a tithe to God's work, concealing or hiding or not declaring income, evading taxes, money laundering, not honoring loans, hustling others or being hustled, or deceiving others or being deceived by con men and women, not repaying lenders, and poor stewardship.

IN JESUS NAME, AMEN! And we forgive all those connected to us by bloodline, covenant and/or contract who have practiced or participated in these things.

Feel free to add anything else to this prayer that the Holy Spirit brings to your mind or spirit in this area of Financial Sins and Mammon. Take as long as you need to deal with this area thoroughly in your ancestral bloodline. When you are finished, turn to the next chapter.

## ENDNOTES

1. *Strong's Greek, 3986, 3803, 1939.*
2. *Strong's Greek, 3126, 2962.*

# PRAYER SESSION NOTES

## CHAPTER 12
# ADDICTIONS AND DYSFUNCTIONS

This is an area that I daresay affects every family and every bloodline in some measure, and far too often in dramatic ways that end in heartache or heartbreak, dysfunctional lives and families, broken homes, shattered dreams, and stolen or lost time—often years or decades. This area of addictions is one of the most insidious and prevalent areas common to human experience. It quite often has debilitating and destructive generational effects, and it takes a strong person to stand in the gap, break the cycle, and repent for the curses, lies, sins, iniquities and transgressions in the ancestral bloodline for this area.

Scripture has much to say about shame, guilt, fear, unrighteous anger, rage, fury, anxiety, worry, lying, deceit, and other addictions. For example, 2 Cor. 7:10 (NIV) says:

> *Godly sorrow brings repentance that leads to salvation and leaves no regret, but worldly sorrow brings death.*

Worldly sorrow would include such things as depression, despair, sadness, sorrow, melancholy, disappointment, disillusionment, despondency, hopelessness, excessive or prolonged grief, mourning, lamentation, weeping, etc.

Fear is another big issue for many people. 1 John 4:18 (NIV) says:

> There is no fear in love. But perfect love drives out fear, because fear has to do with punishment. The one who fears is not made perfect in love.

Rom. 8:15 (NIV) adds:

> The Spirit you received does not make you slaves, so that you live in fear again; rather, the Spirit you received brought about your adoption to sonship. And by him we cry, "Abba, Father."

2 Tim. 1:7 (NLT) states:

> For God has not given us a spirit of fear and timidity, but of power, love, and self-discipline.

John 14:27 (NIV) says:

> Peace I leave with you; my peace I give you. I do not give to you as the world gives. Do not let your hearts be troubled and do not be afraid.

Psa. 34:4 (NIV) notes:

> I sought the Lord, and he answered me; he delivered me from all my fears.

ADDICTIONS AND DYSFUNCTIONS | 167

Psa. 27:1 (NIV) adds:

> The Lord is my light and my salvation—whom shall I fear? The Lord is the stronghold of my life—of whom shall I be afraid?

Psalm 23:4 (BSB, NKJV) says:

> Even though I walk through the valley of the shadow of death, I will fear no evil, for You are with me; Your rod and Your staff, they comfort me.

Psa. 56:3-4 (NIV) records:

> When I am afraid, I put my trust in you. In God, whose word I praise—in God I trust and am not afraid. What can mere mortals do to me?

Psa. 118:6 (NIV) writes:

> The Lord is with me; I will not be afraid. What can mere mortals do to me?

Isa. 54:4 (NIV) says:

> Do not be afraid; you will not be put to shame. Do not fear disgrace; you will not be humiliated. You will forget the shame of your youth and remember no more the reproach of your widowhood.

Matt. 10:28 (NIV) adds:

> "Do not be afraid of those who kill the body but cannot kill the soul. Rather, be afraid of the One who can destroy both soul and body in hell."

Isa. 41:10 (NIV) states:

*"So do not fear, for I am with you; do not be dismayed, for I am your God. I will strengthen you and help you; I will uphold you with my righteous right hand."*

Isa. 41:13 (NIV) notes:

*"For I am the Lord your God who takes hold of your right hand and says to you, Do not fear; I will help you."*

Anxiety and worry are another issue for many people. Psa. 94:19 (NIV) says:

*When anxiety was great within me, your consolation brought me joy.*

Matt. 6:34 (NIV) adds:

*"Therefore do not worry about tomorrow, for tomorrow will worry about itself. Each day has enough trouble of its own."*

1 Pet. 5:6-7 (NIV) reads:

*Humble yourselves, therefore, under God's mighty hand, that he may lift you up in due time. Cast all your anxiety on him because he cares for you.*

Phil. 4:6-7 (NIV) says:

*Do not be anxious about anything, but in every situation, by prayer and petition, with thanksgiving, present your requests to God. And the peace of God, which transcends all understanding, will guard your hearts and your minds in Christ Jesus.*

ADDICTIONS AND DYSFUNCTIONS | 169

Unrighteous, ungodly anger is also a big problem for many people. Jas. 1:19-20 (NIV) says:

> My dear brothers, take note of this: Everyone should be quick to listen, slow to speak and slow to become angry, for man's anger does not bring about the righteous life that God desires.

Psa. 4:4 (NKJV) adds:

> Be angry, and do not sin. Meditate within your heart on your bed, and be still.

The NLT states:

> Don't sin by letting anger control you. Think about it overnight and remain silent.

Eph. 4:26-27 (NLT) writes:

> And "don't sin by letting anger control you." Don't let the sun go down while you are still angry, for anger gives a foothold to the devil.

Eph. 4:31 (NLT) notes:

> Get rid of all bitterness, rage, anger, harsh words, and slander, as well as all types of evil behavior.

Jas. 3:14-18 (NIV) adds:

> But if you harbor bitter envy and selfish ambition in your hearts, do not boast about it or deny the truth. Such "wisdom" does not come down from heaven but is earthly, unspiritual, demonic. For where you have envy and selfish ambition, there you find disorder and every

*evil practice. But the wisdom that comes from heaven is first of all pure; then peace-loving, considerate, submissive, full of mercy and good fruit, impartial and sincere. Peacemakers who sow in peace raise a harvest of righteousness.*

Finally, Satan is a liar and the father of lies, according to John 8:44, and in fact, lying is his native tongue or language. He is well-versed and well-practiced at lying, and is highly skilled; he is a clever, cunning, shrewd craftsman, chameleon and master deceiver. Prov. 6:16-19 (ESV) says:

*There are six things that the Lord hates, seven that are an abomination to him: haughty eyes, a lying tongue, and hands that shed innocent blood, a heart that devises wicked plans, feet that make haste to run to evil, a false witness who breathes out lies, and one who sows discord among brothers.*

1 Pet. 2:1 (NIV) says:

*Therefore, rid yourselves of all malice and all deceit, hypocrisy, envy, and slander of every kind.*

1 Pet. 3:10 (NIV) adds:

*For whoever would love life and see good days must keep their tongue from evil and their lips from deceitful speech.*

Psa. 5:6 (CSB) states:

*You destroy those who tell lies; the LORD abhors violent and treacherous people.*

Psa. 10:7 (NIV) notes:

> His mouth is full of lies and threats; trouble and evil are under his tongue.

Psa. 36:3 (NIV) writes:

> The words of their mouths are wicked and deceitful; they fail to act wisely or do good.

Psa. 43:1 (NIV) records:

> Vindicate me, my God, and plead my cause against an unfaithful nation. Rescue me from those who are deceitful and wicked.

Psa. 101:7 (NIV) says:

> No one who practices deceit will dwell in my house; no one who speaks falsely will stand in my presence.

Psa. 120:2 (NIV) adds:

> Save me, Lord, from lying lips and from deceitful tongues.

And, Rev. 21:8 (NIV) includes liars in the list of those who will be assigned to the lake of fire:

> But the cowardly, the unbelieving, the vile, the murderers, the sexually immoral, those who practice magic arts, the idolaters and all liars—they will be consigned to the fiery lake of burning sulfur. This is the second death.

Lying and deceit are addictions that you just can't afford; the cost is too high.

I have some personal experience with this area of addictions. While I was blessed to grow up in a home where one of my parents was a Christian, nevertheless, I witnessed, was exposed to, and experienced firsthand, several of the items listed below in the prayer template as a child and teenager. Later, as a young adult, I began a journey of inner healing, completed my education, and eventually became a minister, businessman, author and speaker, husband and father. No matter where you started from in life, or where you came from, you can overcome the past and any generational addictions by choosing to follow and obey Christ, renew your mind (Rom. 12:1-2), sanctify your soul (Lev. 20:7-8; 1 Pet. 2:9-12), and let Him heal you and transform you into His likeness, image and character.

With this in mind, you can begin reading the prayer of repentance below. Please remember that you are testifying as a witness under oath in your own defense in the Courts of Heaven, and this and other prayers which follow in subsequent chapters will become part of the Court record. I invite you to pray this powerful prayer of repentance now.

# REPENT FOR ROOT ISSUES/SINS OF ADDICTIONS/DYSFUNCTIONS AND CLEANSE ANCESTRAL BLOODLINE

## PRAYER TEMPLATE

We renounce and repent of, and cut ties to and break agreement with, all addictions, addictive behaviors and patterns, substances and thoughts, including but not limited to: gambling, cursing, pornography, lust of all kinds, sexual perversion, sexual addictions, substance abuse, drugs, alcohol, tobacco, workaholism, food addictions, overeating, binging, anorexia, bulimia, insomnia, sleep disorders, nightmares or other recurrent bad dreams, trauma, pain, loss, chaos, turmoil, pandemonium, drama, faultfinding, strife, conflict, sadness, melancholy, despair, depression, hopelessness, disappointment, bitterness, hatred, unforgiveness, fear, phobias, panic, terror, anxiety, worry, insecurity, isolation, withdrawal, apathy, indifference, lethargy, fatigue, psychological dysfunction, nervous tics, self-harm, self-sabotage, other dysfunctional or self-destructive behaviors and attitudes, self-centeredness, self-promotion, selfishness, self-loathing/self-hatred, low self-esteem, sefl-abasement, self-condemnation, unworthiness, orphan spirit, victimhood, shame, guilt, defensiveness, masks, escapism, codependency, enablement, self-actualization, pride, arrogance, haughtiness, contempt, condescension, self-exaltation, self-aggrandizement, narcissism, blame, blame-shifting, exaggeration, lying, deception, deceit, denial, control, secrets, passivity, manipulation, performance, perfectionism, rejection, betrayal, abandonment, seeking attention, confusion, distraction, stuffing emotions, deadening or disconnecting from emotions, stoicism, fearing emotions, hating emotions, cursing emotions, out of control emotions, unrighteous anger, rage, fury, volcanic wrath, withholding of love and affection, withholding of affirmation and praise, withholding of acceptance, procrastination, restlessness, hoarding, excessive shopping, compulsive shopping, excessive entertainment, and obsession with or addiction to social media.

IN JESUS NAME, AMEN! And we forgive all those connected to us by bloodline, covenant and/or contract who have practiced or participated in these things.

Feel free to add anything else to this prayer that the Holy Spirit brings to your mind or spirit in this area of Addictions and Dysfunctions. Take as long as you need to deal with this area thoroughly in your ancestral bloodline. When you are finished, turn to the next chapter.

# PRAYER SESSION NOTES

# CHAPTER 13
# RELIGION

Using a military term and analogy, issues and wounds from the Religion area could be called "friendly fire," since they originate in large part from other believers and ministers. Most, or perhaps all of us who have been Christians for any length of time, have been wounded by friendly fire—which comes from a variety of sources and in a variety of forms—such as the tragedy, grief and devastation of a church split, or a major congregational scandal, or a disagreement on a doctrinal or social issue.

Friendly fire also ranges from well-intended Christians who are either lacking social skills or social graces, or are just naive or insensitive, or socially clumsy and awkward, or biblically ignorant or illiterate, to heavy-handed, autocratic bureaucrats in the denominational hierarchy, to senior pastors or bishops who are either insecure and jealous of those more gifted than themselves, or are controlling and not able to delegate, or can preach but not administrate, or vice versa. This also includes doctrinal heresies such as cessationism, universalism, dualism, etc. which are taught by some church leaders and groups today.

Issues such as leadership and communication styles, team-building ability, pulpit presence, vision, budget management, motivational ability, discipline and correction of church members and staff, maturity of character, agape love, humility vs. pride and ego, how to handle and deal with conflict, nepotism, succession, ambition, greed, salary and compensation, performance reviews, legal liability, accounting procedures and tax audits, human resources, recruitment, marketing and branding, online web presence, governance structure, church growth, worship, offerings, fundraising, benevolence, family counseling, children's ministry, youth group, teaching curriculum, and more, all come into play in this area of Religion.

Let's face it. Churches are volunteer organizations, and they suffer from and are subject to, many of the same issues and constraints as other nonprofit organizations. All people have blind spots, including leaders. And, volunteers have issues as well. We are all in the process of being matured, perfected and sanctified.

**ALL PEOPLE HAVE BLIND SPOTS, INCLUDING LEADERS.**

And, of course, throughout Church history, there are many serious issues that have existed, such as sexual abuse of those entrusted to their care by priests, teaching false doctrine for profit such as selling indulgences in the mistaken belief that dead relatives or friends can be prayed out of purgatory or hell and into paradise or heaven, abuses during the Crusades, popes who tried to rule or control nations or kingdoms or secular government in addition to the Catholic Church, religious leaders

RELIGION | 177

who labeled as heretics and excommunicated and/or executed and martyred those whose religious views differed from the established religious party line or dogma of the day, and those who persecuted or killed translators and printers, and other innovators, scholars, scientists, theologians and teachers who were called and anointed of God.

And, during times of war, some clergy remained neutral or silent, went into exile or hiding, and/or looked the other way at abuses and atrocities of populations by various despotic national leaders and rogue governments and political parties, thus tacitly consenting to vandalism, theft, harassment, confiscation of private property, intimidation, coercion, propaganda, murder, torture, illegal detention and imprisonment, gestapo tactics, breaking up of families, lack of due process, genocide, socialism, communism, fascism, state religion, conscription, overthrow or subjugation of the rule of law and legal system and constitutional government with elected representatives.

An excellent example of religious forms and practice and the religious spirit at work in a local church is found in Col. 2:16-23, where Paul and Timothy gave correction and instruction to the church at Colossae regarding this issue. With this in mind, you can begin reading the prayer of repentance that follows now. Please remember that you are testifying as a witness under oath in your own defense in the Courts of Heaven, and this and other prayers which follow in subsequent chapters will become part of the Court record. I invite you to pray this powerful prayer of repentance now.

# REPENT FOR ROOT ISSUES/ SINS OF RELIGION AND CLEANSE ANCESTRAL BLOODLINE

## PRAYER TEMPLATE

We renounce and repent of, and cut ties to and break agreement with, all religious sins, false beliefs and practices, including but not limited to: legalism, formalism, cessationism, universalism, ultimate reconciliation, gnosticism, asceticism, animism, humanism, secularism, dualism, denominationalism, sectarianism, syncretism, inclusivism, agnosticism, atheism, viewing and treating grace as a license to sin, self-righteousness, spiritual pride, critical spirit, religious forms, spirit of offense, doctrines of demons, teachings and doctrines having a form of godliness but denying the power thereof, quenching the Holy Spirit, rites, rituals, human creeds, worship of icons, worship of Mary, worship of saints, worship of angels, worship of false gods or false deities, ancestral worship, idolatry, false religions, cults, apostasy, backsliding, unbelief, blasphemy, heresy, hypocrisy, Phariseeism, spirit of antichrist, spirit of this age, and unholy alliances.

IN JESUS NAME, AMEN! And we forgive all those connected to us by bloodline, covenant and/or contract who have practiced or participated in these things.

Feel free to add anything else to this prayer that the Holy Spirit brings to your mind or spirit in this area of Religion. Take as long as you need to deal with this area thoroughly in your ancestral bloodline. When you are finished, turn to the next chapter.

# PRAYER SESSION NOTES

180 | PRAYERS FOR CLEANSING ANCESTRAL BLOODLINES IN THE COURTS OF HEAVEN

CHAPTER 14

# RACIAL, GENDER, AGE AND CULTURAL BIAS, PREJUDICE, DISCRIMINATION AND PERSECUTION

This area of sin in ancestral bloodlines, has an oversized or disproportionate share of wounds, traumas, tragedies, betrayal, bitterness, heartache, shattered dreams, broken families, revenge, hate, violence, animosity, unforgiveness, stereotyping, bias, prejudice, discrimination and persecution. Racism, sexism, age bias, cultural differences, prejudice and discrimination, create fertile soil and a lush landscape for Satan to have his way with humans, and to incite misunderstanding and distrust. In fact, few areas have as much potential for division, discord, hatred, bitterness, offense, wounds, trauma, misunderstanding, unforgiveness, distrust, suspicion, explosive emotional outbursts, unrighteous anger and violence, as this one.

This is not a new phenomenon, and unfortunately it has existed for thousands of years. Beauty is in the eye of the beholder, and perception is often not reality. All that glitters is not gold, and humans are made in the image of God and are complex beings— much more than race or skin color, than gender or sex, than culture or nation of origin, and more than age. I could list other identifiers here that differentiate and/or group people such as highest level of education completed, socioeconomic status, income level, job or employment status, home ownership status, zip code, military service, religious preference, demographics, psychographics, etc.

Satan was able to tempt and persuade Eve by deceiving her and appealing to the lust of the flesh, the lust of the eyes, and the pride of life. The Devil still uses the same tactics with people today. We have to master our physical senses and learn to realize and accept that we are spirits with a body, not bodies with a spirit. We are new creations in Christ but we are all being transformed, perfected and sanctified in the realm of our soul, which consists of mind, will, and emotions. We are all in process and becoming mature in Christ. We must grow spiritually and renew our minds and train our spirit man to predominate and be in control of our lives, and not our flesh or carnal nature or physical appetites or emotions or feelings. This takes time, dying to self, self-discipline and self-control.

As saints of God, we must learn to celebrate our differences and relate to other cultures, ethnicities and people groups. God did not think it was best for all humans on the earth to live in the same city or region and to speak the same language. You can read this account for yourself of the Tower of Babel and God's intervention in Gen. 11:1-9. As a result, we have different languages, different nations, and different cultures in the earth. God apparently likes diversity, and is an equal opportunity employer. He has the largest family in the world and the universe, since He has adopted each of us as His children, and we are now joint heirs with Christ (John 1:12-13; 2 Cor. 6:18; Rom. 8:14-17; Gal. 4:4-5; Eph. 1:5).

There is an old saying that blood is thicker than water. We all bleed red when cut or shot. Families tend to stick together and defend each other when attacked, even when they disagree with each other at other times. Relationships and loyalties within a family are the strongest and most important ones. And the blood of Jesus and His Holy Spirit unite us together as saints and disciples of Christ. It's essential to be a follower, not just a fan! We have to take up our cross and die daily, and be willing to pay whatever price is required. We are also corporately the body of Christ and the family of God, and the Church global or universal. My friend Dr. Alveda King likes to says, "We are one blood" (Acts 17:26). As the family of God, we learn to love one another as Christ loved us, despite our physical and cultural differences, as we relate to each other by the Spirit and not after the flesh.

With this in mind, you can begin reading the prayer of repentance which follows now. Please remember that you are testifying as a witness under oath in your own defense in the Courts of Heaven, and this and other prayers which follow in subsequent chapters will become part of the Court record. I invite you to pray this powerful prayer of repentance now.

# REPENT FOR ROOT ISSUES/SINS OF RACIAL, GENDER, AGE AND CULTURAL BIAS, PREJUDICE, DISCRIMINATION AND PERSECUTION, AND CLEANSE ANCESTRAL BLOODLINE

## PRAYER TEMPLATE

We renounce and repent of, and cut ties to and break agreement with, all sins of racial, gender, age and cultural bias, prejudice, discrimination and persecution against individuals, people groups and nations, including but not limited to: First Nations Tribes, Indigenous and Aboriginal People Groups, Jews (anti-Semitism), racism, sexism, misogyny, misandry, issues regarding age, bigotry, stereotyping people, hate crimes, ignorance, insensitivity, intolerance, having strong dislike and/or hatred of other people or people groups, having attitudes of superiority or condescension or hostility or condemnation or judgment toward other people or people groups, xenophobia, broken treaties and covenants, moving or changing boundaries, forced dislocation and relocation to other lands, confiscation of lands and property and assets, denying or forbidding or destroying native cultures for other people groups, forcing or requiring formal education and/or a different language for other people groups, having anti-social or sociopathic thoughts and behaviors, and misanthropy.

IN JESUS NAME, AMEN! And we forgive all those connected to us by bloodline, covenant and/or contract who have practiced or participated in these things.

Feel free to add anything else to this prayer that the Holy Spirit brings to your mind or spirit in this area of Racial, Gender, Age and Cultural Bias, Prejudice, Discrimination and Persecution. Take as long as you need to deal with this area thoroughly in your ancestral bloodline. When you are finished, turn to the next chapter.

## PRAYER SESSION NOTES

PRAYERS FOR CLEANSING ANCESTRAL BLOODLINES IN THE COURTS OF HEAVEN

# CHAPTER 15
# SINS OF OMISSION

This last area of repentance focuses on sins of omission, rather than sins of commission—i.e., what you and your family and ancestors could have done, but didn't do, or haven't done for those still living. This area may be more of a blind spot for you than some of the other areas, since it is less obvious in some ways, and not as evident or apparent. It's also a prime area to be open to, have faith for and even to ask God for the recovery of blessings, mantles, gifts, and/or assignments for you and your family during your session, that were available to your ancestors, but that they may have been unaware of, ignored, declined, refused, and/or run away from like Jonah in previous generations.

This area is also a good place to pray to the Lord about your book of purpose and destiny and identity which was written in heaven before you were born, according to Psalm 139. Many people either unknowingly or subconsciously, or at times, even intentionally or because of circumstances and life pressures, choose or accept or settle for a Plan B, C, D or E for their lives that is less than God's best and different than what He has written in their book of purpose and destiny.

It has been well said that nothing is wasted in God's economy, and there is much truth and hope in that. God NOTHING specializes in many things, including grace, love, IS WASTED truth, forgiveness, mercy and redemption, and IN GOD'S because of this, it is never too late to repent ECONOMY. and to choose Plan A while you are still alive. Read the story of the Prodigal Son and the Faithful Father in Luke 15 as a prime example of this. Our God is a God of the second chance, and the second mile.

Now if you are at an advanced age in life, you may not have as much fruit or as big a harvest as you could have had if you had chosen Plan A earlier, but steward well the time you do have left. And, remember that Moses and Caleb began their ministries at age 80, and that God calls and works with imperfect people.

Just tell the Lord that you want His plan for your life, and ask Him to reveal and confirm that to you, and make it possible and open the right doors and provide the right connections and resources, and lead you and guide you each step of the way, and show you what part you need to play and anything that you need to do. Then, be obedient and exercise faith, prayer, diligence, courage and patience. Tell the Lord that you want to fulfill every part of your purpose and destiny on earth. Take a few moments right now and pray that in your own words or from the sentences above. When you are finished, continue reading.

Here are just a few Scriptures to help provide a context and reference for you for this area. Gal. 6:10 (NIV) says:

SINS OF OMISSION | 189

> *Therefore, as we have opportunity, let us do good to all people, especially to those who belong to the family of believers.*

The NKJV states:

> *Therefore, as we have opportunity, let us do good to all, especially to those who are of the household of faith.*

So, if you don't do good to other people when you have the opportunity and hopefully the means to do so, then that would be a sin of omission. 1 Pet. 4:10 (NIV) adds:

> *Each of you should use whatever gift you have received to serve others, as faithful stewards of God's grace in its various forms.*

So, if you don't use your spiritual gift(s) to serve others, that also would be a sin of omission. John 15:12 (NASB) says:

> *"This is My commandment, that you love one another, just as I have loved you."*

Luke 6:31 (NASB) notes:

> *"Treat others the same way you want them to treat you."*

Gal. 6:2 (NASB) writes:

> *Bear one another's burdens, and thereby fulfill the law of Christ.*

So, the converse of these Scriptures would be that if you don't love one another as Christ has loved you, and that if you don't treat others the same way you want them to treat you, and that if you don't bear one another's burdens, that these would be sins of omission, and would be disobeying these commandments of Christ.

One other Scripture that makes this point very clearly is Jas. 4:17. The NIV says,

> If anyone, then, knows the good they ought to do and doesn't do it, it is sin for them.

The ESV adds,

> So whoever knows the right thing to do and fails to do it, for him it is sin.

The BSB notes,

> Anyone, then, who knows the right thing to do, yet fails to do it, is guilty of sin.

And the GNT writes,

> So then, if we do not do the good we know we should do, we are guilty of sin.

That's extremely clear and plain language, but a high hurdle to clear in the race of life. I could cite numerous other Scriptures here, and make similar comparisons and conclusions, but I believe this brief sampling makes the point adequately.

With this in mind, you can begin reading the prayer of repentance that follows now. Please remember that you are testifying as a witness under oath in your own defense in the Courts of Heaven, and this prayer will become part of the Court record. I invite you to pray this powerful prayer of repentance now.

## REPENT FOR ROOT ISSUES/SINS OF OMISSION AND CLEANSE ANCESTRAL BLOODLINE

### PRAYER TEMPLATE

We renounce and repent of, and cut ties to and break agreement with, all sins of omission, including but not limited to: ignoring God, shutting God out, running away from God, saying no to God, not honoring God, not honoring parents, not doing good to others when we had the opportunity and/or means to do so, not praying on a regular or consistent basis, not reading or studying God's word on a regular or consistent basis, not being baptized, not taking communion in a worthy manner or on a regular or consistent basis, not giving financially on a regular or consistent basis, not volunteering or serving in God's kingdom, not forgiving others, not forgiving ourselves, not forgiving God, not accepting or receiving or acknowledging the grace and love and gifts and sonship and inheritance of God, not receiving or acknowledging the Holy Spirit, not accepting or receiving the finished work of Christ on the cross of Calvary (Golgotha), not working as unto the Lord, not loving our neighbor as ourselves, not loving our spouses and families, not loving our enemies, not loving and forgiving those who persecute us or speak evil and slander against us, not loving and forgiving those who betray and/or abandon us, not loving and forgiving those who lie to us and/or abuse us, not pressing into or cooperating with the sanctification process, not pressing on to spiritual maturity in Christ, not modeling the life of Christ to those around us in our spheres of influence, and not being an effective or faithful witness of Christ.

IN JESUS NAME, AMEN! And we forgive all those connected to us by bloodline, covenant and/or contract who have practiced or participated in these things.

Feel free to add anything else to this prayer that the Holy Spirit brings to your mind or spirit in this area of Sins of Omission. Take as long as you need to deal with this area thoroughly in your ancestral bloodline. This concludes the prayers of repentance for the 10 major areas of sin common to all ancestral bloodlines. When you are finished, you can turn to Chapter 16, as we begin Part Three.

# PRAYER SESSION NOTES

PART THREE

# RESTING YOUR CASE AND RECEIVING AND ENFORCING YOUR VERDICT

"FOR IF YOU FORGIVE OTHER PEOPLE WHEN THEY SIN AGAINST YOU, YOUR HEAVENLY FATHER WILL ALSO FORGIVE YOU. BUT IF YOU DO NOT FORGIVE OTHERS THEIR SINS, YOUR FATHER WILL NOT FORGIVE YOUR SINS."

– MATTHEW 6:14-15 (NIV)

## CHAPTER 16
# RESTING YOUR CASE AND RECEIVING YOUR VERDICT

By this time, after praying all the prayers of repentance for the different areas in the previous chapters, you should be feeling a lot lighter and be almost ready to rest your defense. Before doing so, however, first ask the Holy Spirit, "Is there anything else I need to repent of for myself or my ancestral bloodline, or those joined to us by covenant?" Listen carefully and be led by the Holy Spirit, and your seers, if any. If you have seers with you, ask them if they see anything left on the Devil's side of the Courtroom. It should look pretty empty there by now. Once you and your legal team have dealt with and repented for any final issues identified, if any, at this point you, or Jesus your Advocate, can tell the Judge, "The defense rests, Your Honor."

You are now ready to receive the Judge's verdict in your case. This is the moment you have been waiting for.

Isa. 43:26 (NKJV) says:

> "Put Me in remembrance; Let us contend together; State your case, that you may be acquitted."

This is an invitation to the nation of Israel through the prophet Isaiah in the Old Testament, to contend with God and present their case so that they can be acquitted. That's good news! God wants to acquit you! But, in His role as Judge, He has to be impartial and fair to both sides and follow the governing law, rules of evidence, and other legal principles in His word that apply in the Courts of Heaven. This moment is what you and your legal team have been working toward up to this point in the session.

You have been actively listening to and obeying the Holy Spirit and systematically repenting of sins, iniquities, transgressions, curses and lies in your life and, more importantly, in your ancestral bloodline, and in those joined to you and your bloodline by covenant. Your repentance and Jesus' defense have effectively negated (nullified or disqualified), and/or refuted (disproved) the Devil's evidence against you and your bloodline. Satan's evidence and eyewitness testimony and expert witnesses have all been presented against you from your ancestral bloodline, and he has accused you before God, just as he did with Job in Job 1:6-12 and 2:7-13, and Joshua the high priest in Zech. 3:1-2.

Now it's time to hear from the Judge. After both the prosecution and defense have rested their cases, the Judge delivers a verdict. My team and I typically hear God the holy and impartial Supreme

Judge say something like this as He raises His gavel on the bench to deliver His verdict in your case:

> *"In the matters brought before this Court today for adjudication, in the case of Satan v. Name of Defendant(s), I find and declare Defendant(s) not guilty, and you are free from all accusations and charges against you. This case is dismissed with prejudice."*

If you have trouble hearing and/or seeing God and the Holy Spirit speak to you, you may need to ask your prophetic seers, if any, to describe what they are seeing and hearing in this regard. This verdict of not guilty is obviously a huge cause for celebration and a time for rejoicing and thanksgiving.

I encourage Defendant(s) to pray a short prayer for restoration, recovery, judicial relief and remedy at this point, while the Court is still in session. This prayer is actually a petition that Jesus will present to the Judge on your behalf after you or one of your seers, if any, reads it aloud in the Courtroom, and it is listed for you below. And, although this petition has a formal title and specific legal purpose, my team and I have informally nicknamed it the "Power R's" Petition.

# PETITION FOR JUDICIAL RELIEF AND REMEDY

## PRAYER TEMPLATE

Your Honor, now that You have ruled in my/their case and issued a verdict of not guilty for Defendant(s), I/we petition this Court, on behalf of Name of Defendant(s), and ask for Recompense, Reconciliation, Recovery, Refreshing, Rejuvenation, Release, Relief, Remedy, Remuneration, Reparation, Repayment, Replenishment, Restitution, Restoration, Resurrection, Reward, and/or Realignment to be effected, issued and/or granted in any and every form, in any and every amount, and through any means or mechanism of the Court's choosing. I/We remind this Court that Satan has stolen from and otherwise harmed or injured Defendant(s), as was shown and established by the evidence in my/their case, and has caused and/or contributed to significant and substantial losses, including but not limited to a loss of assets, employment, favor, finances, goodwill, health, honor, income, inheritance, jobs, money, opportunity, promotion, property, prosperity, relationships, reputation, resources, respect, rest, sleep, social standing, time and/or wellbeing. Therefore, I/we hereby request of and petition this Court that Satan be ordered to recompense and repay Defendant(s) sevenfold for these losses, as Your word declares in Proverbs 6:31, and that this Petition be granted immediately, without delay, and be so ordered by this Court. IN JESUS' NAME, AMEN."

At this point, my team and I typically hear the Judge say something like this:

**"Defendant's Petition for Judicial Relief and Remedy is hereby granted. This Court is now adjourned."**

Then, as the Courtroom begins to empty out, I like to read and speak Jude 1:24-25 (NASB) over the Defendant(s) as a blessing and thanksgiving declaration:

*Now to Him who is able to keep you from stumbling, and to make you stand in the presence of His glory blameless*

> *with great joy, to the only God our Savior, through Jesus Christ our Lord, be glory, majesty, dominion and authority, before all time and now and forever. Amen.*

If you are going through the session by yourself, you can read this Scripture aloud as an affirmation and praise, or if you have one or more seers with you, one of them can read and speak it aloud over you.

Now, at this point, you should be feeling a whole lot lighter and cleaner than when you started the session(s), and joyous, buoyant, and/or like floating on air. Some of those that my team and I have ministered to in the Courts of Heaven tell us that they feel like they have been to a "spiritual spa," or a spiritual detox, with everything on the inside of them steam cleaned, power washed and the sludge, grime, gunk, dirt, stains and filth removed, and everything inside tuned up and filled up by the Spirit. They also report feeling or sensing that a weight of heaviness has lifted from them during the session.

I never cease to be amazed and even awed by the goodness and grace and love of God and the power and insight and gentleness of the Holy Spirit and the strength and authority and wisdom of Jesus during our sessions in the Courts of Heaven. In addition to the relief, freedom and breakthrough that Defendants experience, some of the people we have ministered to in the Courts of Heaven have reported various spiritual phenomena which have occurred during their sessions. Among these are receiving the baptism of the Holy Spirit, receiving the gift of tongues, receiving physical healing, receiving emotional or inner healing, receiving relational healing, receiving a new or upgraded identity, receiving new spiritual gifts and/or mantles, and having demons/demonic spirits cast out of them and/or their bloodline.

We focus on helping Defendants with ancestral bloodline repentance during our sessions, but these and other spiritual phenomena sometimes occur also, either spontaneously or as the result of a Spirit-led prayer. In one session, a husband wanted to join his wife to pray for their son in the Courts of Heaven, but he was an unbeliever, and so we led him in the sinner's prayer before we started the session and brought him into the kingdom of God before taking him and his wife into the Courts of Heaven.

For another couple who own a medical transportation business, within four months after their session, they had purchased 10 additional vehicles. One pastor in Europe reported that the Sunday following their session, during their morning church service, they saw an increased presence of the glory of God that was tangible. There are many other testimonies that I could share here from our Courts of Heaven alumni, but I will refrain from doing so because of space limitations.

Now, at this point in the sessions that I lead, my team and I and the Defendant(s) are typically escorted by an angel out a side door and down a hallway from this Court to a second and final venue in heaven where we interact with Jesus, the holy angels, and the great Cloud of Witnesses for the last 30 minutes of the session, and minister prophetically to Defendant(s). Just to be clear, we also minister prophetically to Defendant(s) throughout the session as we are led by the Spirit. Typically, the angel has Defendant(s) stop at a Wardrobe Room briefly to receive and change into new garments while enroute to this venue. We call

# RESTING YOUR CASE AND RECEIVING YOUR VERDICT | 201

this next venue the Celebration Hall or the Overcomers Room. It's a party in your honor to celebrate your victory in the Courtroom.

Luke 15:10 (NIV) says that the angels in heaven rejoice at the repentance of one sinner:

> *"In the same way, I tell you, there is rejoicing in the presence of the angels of God over one sinner who repents."*

It is no surprise, then, that the angels would also want to celebrate your victory in the Courts of Heaven. Jesus is there also in this venue to greet you and celebrate with you, and there is usually a receiving line present with some members from the great Cloud of Witnesses to shake your hand or give you a hug or an encouraging word. Some of these may have been in the gallery earlier in your Courtroom session.

Among those we have seen in our sessions over the years from the great Cloud of Witnesses include: Noah, Abraham, Sarah, Joseph, Daniel, David, Esther, Ruth, Naomi, Boaz, Miriam, Moses, Bezalel, Ezekiel, Samuel, Job, Isaiah, Jeremiah, Mary Magdalene, Mary the mother of Jesus, Phoebe, Dorcas, Deborah, Gideon, Joshua, Caleb, Jehu, Paul, Peter, Matthew, John the Beloved, Luke, John Mark, James, Barnabas, Timothy, Titus, Aquila and Priscilla, Silas, Ana, John the Baptist, Lydia, Philip, Philip's four daughters, Cornelius, Zaccheus, Smith Wigglesworth, John G. Lake, Oral Roberts, T.L. Osborn, Kathryn Kuhlman, Amy Semple McPherson, Maria Woodworth-Etter, Bob Jones, John Paul Jackson, Evan Roberts, Billy Graham, Steve Hill and Rees Howells, among others. Sometimes a deceased relative or two of the Defendant(s) will also be in attendance in the gallery. These saints are very much alive in spirit, so this is not necromancy.[1]

Most of the time we see this venue as a large celebration hall filled with overcomers. Often there is music playing and heavenly foods and beverages are there, and a gifts table. We usually hear worship music, and sometimes an orchestra is playing ballroom music. There are a couple of angels with long trumpets to announce Defendant(s) as they arrive. Occasionally, we are directed by the Spirit or an angel to an outdoor venue for this last part of the session to celebrate, and over the years we have been in gardens, meadows, next to a waterfall, and several other beautiful places in heaven with Defendants.

But, typically, much the same thing happens in this portion of the session no matter which venue we happen to be in on any given day. Jesus greets the Defendant(s) first, and talks to them briefly and congratulates and commends them, and then the holy angels usually bestow some ribbons and medals on the Defendant(s), and then Defendant(s) receives a jeweled crown, a jeweled scepter, a gold necklace with a medallion is placed around their neck, and a royal robe is placed around their shoulders. Then members of the great Cloud of Witnesses congratulate Defendant(s). Finally, my team and I minister prophetically to Defendant(s) regarding their purpose, destiny and identity, and then we each give our closing statements.

Sometimes we pray a Father's Blessing and/or a Mother's Blessing over the Defendant(s), depending on the needs of the Defendant(s) and their past history. Sometimes Holy Spirit will give us a song or a Scripture to release as well. And, almost always, we end in prayer. We want to give thanks to the Lord for all He has done in the session, and for His goodness and mercy and love for us. It is Spirit-led from start to finish. The presence of the Lord is typically very thick and tangible in these sessions in the Courts of Heaven.

By this time, typically the Defendant(s) has been profoundly affected, and/or is undone spiritually. Several Defendants have even told us spontaneously, "I am undone." That is a good thing. It means God has touched or affected or impacted them deeply, like Isaiah, who uttered these same words in Isa. 6:5 many centuries ago. We then give Defendant(s) the opportunity to give us their feedback on the session and any closing statement they want to share with God or my team and I before we close. Then we end the session by sealing everything that was done in the blood of Jesus, say our goodbyes, and we leave the Courts of Heaven with hearts full of joy, thanksgiving, gratitude and praise. Now we turn to Chapter 17.

## ENDNOTE

1. Speaking with or listening to members of the great Cloud of Witnesses while in the Courts of Heaven is not necromancy (which means communicating with the dead in order to predict the future). Many of these saints in heaven are listed in Hebrews 11 and other books of the Bible, and they are very much alive in the Spirit. As I discussed in some detail in Chapter 2, it is our spirit which is able to be in heaven, according to Eph. 2:5-6. Even Jesus, Peter, James and John interacted with deceased saints Moses and Elijah while on the Mount of Transfiguration. See also Robert Henderson, *The Cloud of Witnesses in the Courts of Heaven*, 2019, Shippensburg, PA: Destiny Image Publishers, Inc., Rick Joyner, *The Final Quest*, 1997, New Kensington, PA: Whitaker House, and Dr. Luc Niebergall, *The Heart of Heaven: A Prophetic Encounter*, 2023, Calgary, AB Canada: The Author.

# PRAYER SESSION NOTES

CHAPTER 17

# WALKING OUT AND ENFORCING YOUR VERDICT

Now that you have received your verdict from God, the Supreme Judge, you will need to walk it out in your daily life and enforce it with the enemy. It's one thing to get free. It's quite another to stay free.

Rev. 12:11 (NKJV) says:

*And they overcame him by the blood of the Lamb and by the word of their testimony, and they did not love their lives to the death.*

You now have a testimony of not only what Jesus did for you on the cross, but in the Courts of Heaven. Remind Satan of that the next time he tries to bother you again, if he ever does. You are no longer low-hanging fruit for him, and in fact, you not only have the blood of Jesus speaking for you, but you have a verdict of not guilty from God the just and impartial Supreme Judge in the Courts of Heaven. You won!

Paul the Apostle says in Gal. 5:1 (NIV):

*It is for freedom that Christ has set us free. Stand firm, then, and do not let yourselves be burdened again by a yoke of slavery.*

The MSG states:

*Christ has set us free to live a free life. So take your stand! Never again let anyone put a harness of slavery on you.*

The NLT adds:

*So Christ has truly set us free. Now make sure that you stay free, and don't get tied up again in slavery to the law.*

And the TPT writes:

*Let me be clear, the Anointed One has set us free—not partially, but completely and wonderfully free! We must always cherish this truth and stubbornly refuse to go back into the bondage of our past.*

You need to cherish, nurture and defend your freedom! You have been set free from any outstanding sin issues in your ancestral bloodline, and those doors and legal access points have been closed to the enemy, but you still have to walk out your newly increased level of freedom. Satan may try to test you to see if you really believe it, and if you have really changed your thinking and put on the mind of Christ. Just remember, Satan is a deceiver, and a liar, and the Father of lies. Don't listen to him or agree with him or his demons for even one second if they try to contact you again in the future. Just say "No!" Satan has no authority or influence over you any longer, except what you give him. So, don't give him any ground or room to operate—not even an inch!

Stand your ground in the Spirit realm by faith. 1 Cor. 15:58 (NIV) says:

> *Therefore my dear brothers and sisters, stand firm. Let nothing move you. Always give yourself fully to the work of the Lord, because you know that your labor in the Lord is not in vain.*

Eph. 6:10-11, 13 (ESV) adds:

> *Finally, be strong in the Lord, and in the strength of his might. Put on the whole armor of God, that you may be able to stand against the wiles of the devil ... Therefore take up the whole armor of God, that you may be able to withstand in the evil day, and having done all, to stand firm.*

2 Thess. 2:15 (CSB) notes:

> *So then, brothers and sisters, stand firm and hold to the traditions you were taught, whether by what we said or what we wrote.*

Satan is a three-time loser. In the U.S. criminal justice system, felons with three felony convictions are labeled as habitual offenders or career criminals and typically sentenced to a life of incarceration and imprisonment with no hope of parole. Three strikes and you're out! Well, that applies to Satan as well as felons and baseball. First, God and His holy angels defeated Satan and his rebellion in heaven and kicked Satan and his angelic followers out of heaven permanently.

Second, Jesus defeated Satan at the cross and brought back the keys to death, hell, and hades. Col. 2:15 (NIV) says:

*And having disarmed the powers and authorities, he made a public spectacle of them, triumphing over them by the cross.*

The NKJV adds:

*Having disarmed principalities and powers, He made a public spectacle of them, triumphing over them in it.*

Third, you repented and confessed your sins, and accepted Jesus as your Lord and Savior and invited Him to come into your heart. And now, you and Jesus have won a legal victory against Satan and his demons in the Courts of Heaven.

Even with Jesus, when Satan tried to tempt Him on a high mountain, and showed Him the kingdoms of this world, and offered Him power, position, influence, fame, and fortune (money, riches), Jesus turned down his offer and answered him with the word of God, *"It is written ... "* You can do the same. Luke 4:13 (NIV) says:

*When the devil had finished tempting Jesus, he left him until the next opportunity came.*

Most translations say, *"until an opportune time."* That time came in the Garden of Gethsemane. Jesus said to His disciples in John 14:30 (NKJV):

WALKING OUT AND ENFORCING YOUR VERDICT | 209

> *"I will no longer talk much with you, for the ruler of this world is coming, and he has nothing in me."*

You also can tell Satan now if he dares to contact you again:

> **"You have nothing in me."**

This last verse is actually referring to a legal claim. The AMP says:

> *"I will not speak with you much longer, for the ruler of the world (Satan) is coming. And he has no claim on Me [no power over Me nor anything that he can use against Me]."*

The MSG is similar:

> *"I'll not be talking with you much more like this because the chief of this godless world is about to attack. But don't worry—he has nothing on me, no claim on me."*

In other words, there was no sin found in Jesus that Satan could exploit and use against Him and accuse or charge Him with. You can also tell Satan now if he dares to contact you again:

> **"You have no claim on me, my family, or my bloodline. And, I have a verdict of not guilty from God the Supreme Judge to prove it."**

You can also resist the Devil and he will flee. Resistance training is some of the best strength building training you can do for your physical body; isometrics is one such example. You can also exercise your spiritual muscles. The word "resist" in the Greek is *antistēte*, from the root *anthistémi*, meaning: "to set against, withstand, oppose, resist."[1]

Jas. 4:7-8 (NKJV) says:

*Therefore submit to God. Resist the devil and he will flee from you. Draw near to God and He will draw near to you. Cleanse your hands, you sinners; and purify your hearts, you double-minded.*

The NLT adds:

*So humble yourselves before God. Resist the devil, and he will flee from you. Come close to God, and God will come close to you. Wash your hands, you sinners; purify your hearts, for your loyalty is divided between God and the world.*

The TPT notes:

*So then, surrender to God. Stand up to the devil and resist him and he will turn and run away from you. Move your heart closer and closer to God, and he will come even closer to you. But make sure you cleanse your life, you sinners, and keep your heart pure and stop doubting.*

The MSG writes (author's emphasis):

*So let God work his will in you.* **Yell a loud no to the Devil and watch him scamper. Say a quiet yes to God and he'll be there in no time.** *Quit dabbling in sin. Purify your inner life. Quit playing the field. Hit bottom, and cry your eyes out. The fun and games are over. Get serious, really serious. Get down on your knees before the Master; it's the only way you'll get on your feet.*

WALKING OUT AND ENFORCING YOUR VERDICT | 211

Finally, be diligent and even ruthless in enforcing your victory and freedom in Christ with the enemy. There is an ongoing price to pay for your freedom, which is vigilance and sober-mindedness. Pay it willingly, readily and cheerfully. Tit. 2:12 (KJV) states:

> *Teaching us that, denying ungodliness and worldly lusts, we should live soberly, righteously, and godly in the present age.*

1 Pet. 1:13 (NKJV) says:

> *Therefore gird up the loins of your mind, be sober, and rest your hope fully upon the grace that is to be brought to you at the revelation of Jesus Christ.*

The NIV notes:

> *Therefore, with minds that are alert and fully sober, set your hope on the grace to be brought to you when Jesus Christ is revealed at his coming.*

1 Pet. 5:8-9 (NKJV) adds:

> *Be sober, be vigilant; because your adversary the devil, walks about like a roaring lion, seeking whom he may devour. Resist him, steadfast in the faith, knowing that the same sufferings are experienced by your brotherhood in the world.*

The NIV says:

> *Be alert and of sober mind. Your enemy the devil prowls around like a roaring lion looking for someone to devour. Resist him, standing firm in the faith, because you know*

*that the family of believers throughout the world is undergoing the same kind of sufferings.*

In closing, Rom. 13:12 (NKJV) states:

*The night is far spent, the day is at hand. Therefore, let us cast off the works of darkness, and let us put on the armor of light.*

You can make Satan sorry that he ever came in contact with you or tried to tempt, steal from, deceive or lie to you or your family. Make him pay a high price for the loss, pain, misery and suffering he has caused you and your family over the years. It's payback time, and I am not talking about revenge or vengeance, as that belongs exclusively to the Lord.

I am talking about taking back first in the spirit and then in the natural, what legally belongs to you as a child of God, that the Devil has blocked, hindered, delayed and/or stolen from you, including: identity, relationships, dreams, destiny, a bright future, health, money, riches, wealth, inheritance, honor, favor, promotion, friends, rest, sleep, peace, joy, strength, purpose and much more. Enjoy your new life! Now we turn to Chapter 18.

## ENDNOTE

1. *Strong's Greek, 436.*

CHAPTER 18

# ONGOING MAINTENANCE & REPENTANCE FOR ANY NEW ISSUES THAT MAY ARISE

As we begin this chapter, I commend you for your courage, tenacity and perseverance in taking this journey with me—whether from desperation, curiosity, or spiritual hunger—and doing the repentance work for your ancestral bloodline in the previous chapters. As they say in the hair business regarding washing hair, "wash, rinse and repeat" for any new sins that may occur after receiving your verdict in the Courts of Heaven. This would include any new sins for you personally, and any new sins in your ancestral bloodline that you become aware of for relatives who are currently living, or for anyone that you or your bloodline are in covenant with through business or other associations or strategic alliances.

The good news is that you will not have to revisit sins or curses of the past for yourself or your ancestral bloodline starting from the date of your verdict in the Courts of Heaven and going backward in time, since those have been repented of and dealt with already. So, any future sessions will be much shorter by comparison. Try to live your life so that you keep short accounts and a clean slate with God and other people. Deal with any new issues immediately or within 24 hours when they arise or occur, rather than waiting an extended time to process them.

Be quick to repent, forgive, obey and pray. Try to do this immediately, if possible, but at least within 24 to 48 hours of a sin occurrence, episode or event. Don't let dirty laundry pile up in your life either naturally or spiritually, since it begins to stink and emit a foul-smelling odor after a few days or a week. Stay on top of it and out in front of it, and work to cultivate, develop, and make this a habit and spiritual discipline. It will serve you well.

You may also want to speak and pray a modified version of the Power R's Petition from Chapter 16 over yourself on a daily basis until you see breakthrough. A sample prayer is included below:

*"Lord, I thank you for my verdict from the Supreme Judge in the Courts of Heaven, and I ask for Recompense, Reconciliation, Recovery, Refreshing, Rejuvenation, Release, Relief, Remedy, Remuneration, Reparation, Repayment, Replenishment, Restitution, Restoration, Resurrection, Reward, and/or Realignment to be effected, issued and/or granted to and for me in any and every form, in any and every amount, and through any means or mechanism of heaven's choosing. Amen."*

In addition, try to practice spiritual disciplines on a frequent or regular basis—daily or weekly, if possible, or at least monthly—including prayer, Bible study, fellowship with the saints, quiet time with the Lord to listen and journal and ask Him questions, fasting, giving, communion, stewarding your gifts and serving others, reading books, attending conferences, listening to podcasts and live streamed or archived events, sharing your testimony, and witnessing to the lost. And, if possible, seek out a spiritual mentor to help you in your journey.

Again, be quick to repent, forgive, obey and pray. Let those become rapid responses. When you can do these things consistently, naturally, and voluntarily, out of spiritual hunger and a godly desire to be more like Christ, you are well on your way to spiritual maturity and the ability to maintain and increase your level of freedom in the Spirit.

When you reach this point in your spiritual journey, you may also want to consider becoming a spiritual mentor for others, as the Holy Spirit leads and confirms. This type of role can be challenging at times but also extremely rewarding. It has been well said by many that we need both vertical and horizontal relationships, and that we need to have peers, mentors, and disciples, as the early church leaders did.

This book has been presented conceptually and logistically as one continuous session of several hours in length. In actual practice, my team and I see these sessions range from 4.5 hours to 5.5 hours in duration. It will no doubt take longer than that to read this book and pray the prayers of repentance included herein, and some may want or need to break this up into several shorter sessions rather than one longer session for various reasons. Both approaches are acceptable, and it is more a matter of personal preference. I find it simpler and more convenient, and experience a better flow of the Holy Spirit, to have one longer session. But, I am aware of some other Courts of Heaven navigators and teams who prefer to have multiple sessions with a Defendant(s). Either approach can be effective and fruitful.

This book has also been focused primarily on assisting individuals, married or engaged couples, and families with repenting for their ancestral bloodlines in the Courts of Heaven. Families are the building blocks of society and culture, and strong, healthy families are the key to God's plan for the earth, for the Church, and for His kingdom. God understands and practices generational inheritance and legacy. We would do well to learn from and follow after His example and pattern, and in so doing, our families will become stronger, wiser, healthier and wealthier, and have more influence and impact. As we turn now to Chapter 19, we will discuss briefly how these prayers of repentance can be adapted for use in and by organizations, cities, counties, states, regions and nations.

CHAPTER 19
# PRAYING FOR ORGANIZATIONS, CITIES, COUNTIES, STATES, REGIONS AND NATIONS

Many other audiences need and can benefit from these prayers of repentance as well, such as businesses and corporations, government entities and agencies, including cities, counties, states or provinces, regions, and nations; and nonprofit organizations of all types, including churches, Christian camps, parachurch ministries, colleges and universities, schools and academies, school systems, university systems, think tanks, research institutes, hospitals and health care systems, charitable foundations, endowments, charities, Chambers of Commerce, museums, libraries, art galleries, missions groups, NGOs and more.

Much of this book can be adapted for usage by such entities, and my team and I have led sessions on multiple occasions for businesses and corporations to great effect in the Courts of Heaven, with the CEO and/or owners participating. It is certainly true that organizations do not have eternal souls and ancestral bloodlines, and therefore differ in those important aspects from humans, but they do have histories, missions, cultures, ecosystems, employees, and leaders, as well as shareholders, stakeholders and/or constituents, depending on the type of organization or agency.

God loves families, but He also loves organizations, cities, states, provinces, regions and nations, because they all are made up of people, and they all have purpose and destiny. Jesus wept over Jerusalem, for example, and God loves His people with a steadfast, everlasting love (Psa. 103:17; Jer. 31:3). The Church is called the bride of Christ, and Jesus loves the Church and gave himself up for her to make her holy just as husbands are to love their wives as their own bodies (Eph. 5:22-30). God has also wept over and been jealous for and angry with and disciplined and brought judgment upon His covenant people and the nation of Israel at various times throughout history.

There are other benefits to repentance besides forgiveness and freedom; there is also favor. My team and I have witnessed and observed, and/or received reports and testimonies of fairly dramatic shifts and breakthroughs occurring with some of those to whom we have ministered in the Courts of Heaven. One desperate mother stood in proxy and prayed for her son who was struggling and being verbally abused and harassed in the military by the corporal and sergeant in authority over him, and within 24

PRAYING FOR ORGANIZATIONS, CITIES, COUNTIES, STATES, REGIONS & NATIONS | 219

hours, he had met with a military chaplain and been reassigned to a different unit with enlisted personnel who affirmed and accepted him and were civil, respectful and humane.

Another person that we ministered to in the Courts of Heaven shared this testimony about the effect and fruit of their session.

I can attest to the validity of this ministry as being biblically sound, partly in the fact that I have been miraculously set free, just like with the people whom Jesus healed and set free some two thousand years ago. I've had many physical, emotional and mental health issues over the years, only for them to grow worse as I grew older. After my Courts of Heaven session, most of these issues were completely gone, and the remaining issues are lessening by the day.

As we all know, change is a process and life is a journey. But, I felt the obstacles that had kept me from this lasting change and freedom, were completely removed in the Courts of Heaven. Only through true repentance, can the Lord release to us the freedom that comes only from Him. And, true repentance is a condition of the heart, that bows to the Lordship of Jesus Christ.

Finally, in addition to my healing and freedom, I also received several job offers after my session and accepted a new job that pays me more money and is the dream job I have been praying for.

We also prayed with one entire family—first the father and mother had individual COH sessions, and then they were so impacted and blessed that they requested my team and I to have sessions with each of their teen-aged and adult children. Bradley and Melody Van Peursem from Seattle, WA shared this testimony:

> Before becoming aware of our ancestral/generational bloodline issues, we were struggling as a family, with several members who had long-term chronic health issues, which were adversely affecting both our work and personal lives, and robbing us of finances with lower income and staggering medical expenses. The doctors were stumped and there were no real answers.
>
> When each family member entered a Courts of Heaven (COH) session, immediately the seers identified clear and common patterns/strongholds that needed to be addressed. It was shocking to see and realize the negative impact that our ancestral bloodline sins had been having on our family. Each one of us began repenting of personal sins as well as the sins in our bloodlines, and only then we began to see their power broken. Everything that was stuck began progressing and changing for the better.
>
> Major health answers and breakthroughs have become routine and we now see our lives confirming what Scripture says, rather than defying it. Now that all of us have had our ancestral/generational bloodline issues completely resolved and removed, each generation in our family going forward can live free from the devastating influence of the sins, lies and curses of our forefathers. We are each experiencing growth in our personal desire and passion as believers, and better able to make a difference in the world and fulfill God's original purpose and destiny for our lives.

## BUSINESS CASE STUDY

In one Courts of Heaven session my team and I had with three business principals and owners, they had their backs up against the wall and were facing the prospect of losing their largest customer—a multi-billion-dollar national organization that was threatening to end their multi-year business relationship and pull out of a large contract that had made Defendants profitable. All of this was because of fraud in the form of a kickback scheme that two of their employees had committed in secret in collusion with an employee of their client, without the knowledge or agreement of either the owners or the client.

After the owners took responsibility in the realm of the Spirit and repented on behalf of their negligence and the sins of their employees, as well as the sins of the client's employee, and dealt with these issues in prayer, and forgave the parties involved, and prayed for and blessed their client, the very next day while on a conference call with their client, the whole attitude and atmosphere and situation began to turn around. The client imposed some milestones, timelines and penalties, but agreed to remain as a client and to continue their business contract. This client relationship and their business contract was worth potentially millions of dollars to the owners.

## PRAYING FOR ORGANIZATIONS

To prepare for a business session, I would ask those requesting the session, or Defendant(s), to have a personal session first in the Courts of Heaven to take care of any personal sins and ancestral bloodline issues. Then, they are free to focus on the business history, business issues, financial statements and/or pro forma, mission, goals and objectives, SWOT analysis, and any sins related or connected to the business, in the next session once the owners and/or CEO have dealt with and repented for their personal sins and the sins in their ancestral bloodlines. If the business has access to prophetic seers, the CEO and/or owners could then lead a session for the organization, using this book and their experience from their own personal session as a guide.

Again, you can have a session without seers, but it is more difficult. And again, as I stated earlier in great detail in Chapter 2, I believe it is necessary that individuals have a saving relationship with Jesus in order to access the Courts of Heaven, and so my team and I only conduct sessions with born-again disciples of Jesus Christ. This can be a prime opportunity for desperate executives or leaders in crisis to find salvation and begin a relationship with the Lord Jesus, or rededicate and recommit their lives to Him if they are backslidden. Of course, wise leaders choose to have a Courts of Heaven session when times are good as a preemptive and proactive measure, both for themselves and their organizations.

**INDIVIDUALS NEED A SAVING RELATIONSHIP WITH JESUS IN ORDER TO ACCESS THE COURTS OF HEAVEN.**

Similarly, we would use, and I would recommend, this same strategy for nonprofit organizations, where we would first pray for one or more leaders with some measure of authority in and for the organization—typically the President, Executive Director, Board Chair, and possibly a few Directors and/or Trustees—who also have a saving relationship with Jesus Christ, by scheduling a personal session for them in the Courts of Heaven as a first step.

Then, we would focus on the organization's history and mission, operational issues and challenges, financial statements, goals and objectives, SWOT analysis, and any sins related or connected to the organization, in the next session once these leaders have dealt with and repented for their personal sins and the sins in their ancestral bloodlines. If the organization has access to prophetic seers, then one or more of these executives could lead a session for the organization, using this book and their experience from their own personal session as a guide. You can also have a session without seers, but it is more difficult.

# CASE STUDY FOR A CITY

We have also led sessions for several cities and a few nations in the Courts of Heaven. One such session was in August 2017 for the City of Portland, Oregon and the surrounding region. James Autry and I had discussed the potential benefits of having such a session for several months prior to this, and he had agreed to lead and organize a delegation from his city to represent the city spiritually and governmentally. James is the Executive Director & Community Collaborator for Serving Our Neighbors (SON), an umbrella, city-wide, nonprofit organization which connects leaders of churches, ministries and Christian businesses in the Greater Portland metropolitan area. James and SON help promote and host events throughout the city and region, and he serves in other ways by leading weekly prayer meetings and gatherings with intercessors to pray for the City of Portland.

We set a date and I brought a team of five seers to join with his team of 10 leaders, and co-led the session. James's delegation included an African American bishop, Hispanic pastor, business owners, intercessors, a government leader, and an Asian-

American leader. We also had two members of the Blackfoot tribe in the audience who shared comments from time to time, as they preferred to be in the audience rather than on the panel. It was an amazing and anointed session for three and a half hours, and we even had about 50 local Christians in the audience who were interested in what we were doing.

We appointed a leader to be the court reporter to take notes of what was said during the session, and she filled up five pages of a legal notepad (8.5 x 14 inches) of sins in the history of the city and greater Portland area, going back several centuries to Native American/First Nations time. The 10 local leaders repented of these sins and even wept over their city, and then we prophesied and decreed destiny and purpose for the city and Portland region. There was a heavy, thick presence of the Spirit in this session.

Eleven months after we had the session, Chris Overstreet and his family moved from Redding, Calif., where he was an outreach leader on staff at Bethel Church, to the greater Portland area and started a ministry named Compassion to Action. In Sept. 2018, Compassion to Action held a city- and region-wide, three-day conference for discipleship training, evangelism and healing which drew 7,500 people to the Oregon Convention Center from 25 nations and 40 states.

Speakers included Bill Johnson, Marilyn Hickey, Todd White, Daniel Kolenda, Chris Overstreet, and many other Christian leaders and worship bands. It was reported that thousands of people were healed and received salvation as teams from the event went out into the city and evangelized over those three days. Autry reported that the atmosphere of the City had changed. What used to be hard ground spiritually and a closed

PRAYING FOR ORGANIZATIONS, CITIES, COUNTIES, STATES, REGIONS & NATIONS | 225

atmosphere, has now become fertile soil and an open heaven spiritually. A similar event was repeated again in Sept. 2019 with similar results. Future events are also planned.

According to Autry, "Many prayer leaders have been prayer walking the streets of Portland for 30+ years! Our Prayer-walking SWAT (See What Agreement Transforms) Team began meeting every Saturday morning in September of 2015 to agree with the book of destiny that God had written for the City of Portland. We also intentionally released His shalom and forgiveness over the citizens of our city and region, asking God to release His lovingkindness in order to lead them to repentance. It was based upon this foundation that we then entered into the Courts of Heaven with Dr. Bruce Cook and his team in August of 2017 to legally deal with the issues that had been manifesting in our city and region.

"It was amazing to watch," Autry added, "how the Holy Spirit directed the right people to be in the session, representing the seven major spheres of influence in our city, as well as the 8th Mountain of the Lord. We definitely felt God's presence throughout the session and specifically as acts of obedience were done and decrees were made. It was a game changer for us! We know that this session was the next piece of the puzzle that God had released for such a time as this and it continued to open the door even wider for what God is doing in our city and region. Our pastors, churches, intercessors and business leaders are more united now."

IT WAS AMAZING TO WATCH HOW THE HOLY SPIRIT DIRECTED THE RIGHT PEOPLE TO BE IN THE COURTS OF HEAVEN SESSION.

# A MODEL OF CORPORATE PRAYER FROM 2 CHRON. 7:14

These same prayers also work with states, provinces, regions, and nations. I have prayed on site in the Courts of Heaven in several cities in western Canada, in northern Iraq, and in several large cities in Taiwan. While in Taiwan in May 2019, the presence and glory of the Lord appeared and manifested in a tangible way. In one service, some 800 people were in attendance and after an extended time of teaching and corporate repentance, all were touched by the power of God and the Holy Spirit. In another service, around 500 people were present and many of those were also touched by the power of God and the Holy Spirit.

Earlier in my ministry, before I became aware of the Courts of Heaven, I traveled and ministered in Canada, Mexico, Bolivia, Peru, the United Kingdom, the Netherlands and other places. I have also prayed in the U.S. Supreme Court chambers, the U.S. Congress, the National Press Club, the United Nations, and the House of Representatives and Senate chambers in the State of Washington and the State of Texas, and in many other strategic locations, which shall remain nameless and confidential.

God has provided us with a clear blueprint for effecting and experiencing corporate transformation on a city, state, provincial, regional or national level. After Solomon had dedicated the temple and the glory of the Lord filled it, the Lord appeared to him at night and spoke to Solomon as recorded in 2 Chron. 7:12-22. Verses 13-14 (NIV) say:

> *"When I shut up the heaven so that there is no rain, or command locusts to devour the land or send a plague among my people, if my people, who are called by my*

*name, will humble themselves and pray and seek my face and turn from their wicked ways, then will I hear from heaven and will forgive their sin and will heal their land."*

Note the corporate nature of this Scripture: *"my people ... humble themselves ... their wicked ways ... their sin ... their land."* Second, notice the conditional nature of this Scripture: *"if ..., then ..."* There is a direct cause and effect relationship between their attitudes and actions, and God's response in forgiving their sins and healing their land.

Four steps are mentioned as necessary for God's people as a body or ekklesia in a geographical area to witness and experience corporate transformation: 1) humble themselves, 2) pray, 3) seek God's face, and 4) turn from their wicked ways. Other than the Lord's Prayer in Matt. 6:6-13 as a model for personal prayer, the Church has been offered very few models of how to pray corporately, or for transformation. I humbly suggest and recommend the prayer templates in this book, including the one below, as a possible model for corporate prayer to transform families, organizations, cities, counties, states, regions, nations and continents.

# DECLARATION OF BLESSING FOR A FAMILY, ORGANIZATION, CITY, COUNTY, STATE, REGION, NATION OR CONTINENT

## SCRIPTURAL AUTHORITY FOR DECLARATION:

*"You will also declare a thing, And it will be established for you; So light will shine on your ways." (Job 22:28, NKJV)*

Just as God desires for us to experience and walk in personal transformation by aligning with His foundations of righteousness and justice in our lives (Psa. 37:5-6), He has also provided us with a clear blueprint for effecting and experiencing corporate transformation in a family, organization, city, county, state, region, nation, or continent. 2 Chron. 7:13-14 says, "When I shut up the heaven so that there is no rain, or command locusts to devour the land or send a plague among my people, if my people, who are called by my name, will humble themselves and pray and seek my face and turn from their wicked ways, then will I hear from heaven and will forgive their sin and will heal their land." Note the corporate nature of this Scripture: "my people, humble themselves, their wicked ways, their sin, their land." Second, notice the conditional nature of this Scripture: "if..., then..." There is a direct cause and effect relationship between their attitudes and actions, and God's response in forgiving their sins and healing their land. Four steps are mentioned as necessary for us to witness and experience corporate transformation: 1) humble themselves, 2) pray, 3) seek God's face, and 4) turn from their wicked ways.

> "[F]or all have sinned and fall short of the glory of God," (Rom. 3:23, NKJV)

> "If we confess our sins, He is faithful and just to forgive us our sins and to cleanse us from all unrighteousness." (1 John 1:9, NKJV)

> "Whoever conceals their sins does not prosper, but the one who confesses and renounces them finds mercy." (Prov. 28:13, NIV)

*"Speak and act as those who are going to be judged by the law that gives freedom, because judgment without mercy will be shown to anyone who has not been merciful. Mercy triumphs over judgment." (James 2:12-13, NIV)*

*"But go and learn what this means: 'I desire mercy, not sacrifice.' For I have not come to call the righteous, but sinners." (Matt. 9:13, NIV)*

*"Let us then approach God's throne of grace with confidence, so that we may receive mercy and find grace to help us in our time of need." (Heb. 4:16, NIV)*

# PREAMBLE/INTRODUCTION:

Whereas, You O Sovereign Lord of Hosts and God of Angel Armies, desire that Your Kingdom come, Your will be done, on earth as it is in heaven (Matt. 6:10), and

Whereas, we serve a glorious King and an eternal, everlasting Kingdom that cannot be shaken or destroyed, and this Kingdom was cut out of a mountain but without human hands and all nations will stream to it in the last days (Dan. 2:44-46, Heb. 12:28, Isa. 2:1-5, Mic. 4:1-5), and

Whereas, "The earth will be filled with the knowledge of the glory of the Lord as the waters cover the sea" (Hab. 2:14), and

Whereas, "The glory of the latter house shall be greater than of the former [house]" (Hag. 2:9), and

Whereas, Jesus said, "All authority has been given to Me in heaven and on earth. Go therefore and make disciples of all the nations, baptizing them in the name of the Father and of the Son and of the Holy Spirit, teaching them to observe all things that I have commanded you; and lo, I am with you always, even to the end of the age." And Jesus has delegated His authority to us (Matt. 28:18-20, Mark 16:17-18), and

Whereas, God sent the Comforter, the Holy Spirit, to be with us and live in us to help guide and direct and teach us and intercede for us and enable us to hear directly from Him (John 10:10, John 14:26, 1 Cor. 2:9-16, Rom. 8:28-29), and

Whereas, we are adopted as sons into the family of God and are joint heirs with Christ and are sealed by His Spirit of promise as a firstfruits or guarantee of our eternal inheritance in Christ (Eph. 1:13, Gal. 4:6, Rom. 8:12-17), and

Whereas, "Those who know their God shall do mighty exploits or deeds" (Dan. 11:32), and

Whereas, Jesus told His disciples they would do even greater works than Him (John 14:12), and

Whereas, The Church is the Ekklesia, the called out ones, the saints of God, who Christ died for and is the head of, and

Whereas, "His divine power has given us all things that pertain to life and godliness, through the knowledge of Him who called us by glory and virtue" (2 Pet. 1:3, NKJV), and

Whereas, we are His workmanship, created in Christ Jesus for good works, which God prepared beforehand so that we would walk in them" (Eph. 2:10, NASB), and

Whereas, "The Lord is not slack concerning His promise, as some count slackness, but is longsuffering toward us, not willing that any should perish, but that all should come to repentance" (2 Pet. 3:9, NKJV), and

Whereas, "The Lord is gracious and compassionate, slow to anger and rich in love" (Psa. 145:8, 103:8, NKJV), and

Whereas, "The steadfast love of the Lord never ceases; His mercies never come to an end; they are new every morning; great is Your faithfulness" (Lam. 3:22-23), and

Whereas, the Lord has plans to prosper you and me, and not to harm us, plans to give us a hope and a future (Jer. 29:11, NIV), and

Whereas, "The angel of the Lord encamps all around those who fear Him, And delivers them. Oh, taste and see that the Lord is good; Blessed is the man who trusts in Him! Oh, fear the Lord, you His saints! There is no want to those who fear Him. The young lions lack and suffer hunger; But those who seek the Lord shall not lack any good thing." (Psa. 37:7-10), and

Whereas, "The eyes of the Lord are on the righteous, And His ears are open to their cry...The righteous cry out, and the Lord hears, And delivers them out of all their troubles. The Lord is near to those who have a broken heart, And saves such as have a contrite spirit. Many are the afflictions of the righteous, But the Lord delivers him out of them all. He guards all his bones; Not one of them is broken." (Psa. 37:15, 17-20), and

Whereas, "The Lord is my shepherd; I shall not want. He makes me to lie down in green pastures; He leads me beside the still waters. He restores my soul; He leads me in the paths of righteousness For His name's sake. Yea, though I walk through the valley of the shadow of death, I will fear no evil; For You are with me; Your rod and Your staff, they comfort me. You prepare a table before me in the presence of my enemies; You anoint my head with oil; My cup runs over. Surely goodness and mercy shall follow me All the days of my life; And I will dwell in the house of the Lord Forever." (Psa. 23:1-6), and

Whereas, "He who dwells in the secret place of the Most High Shall abide under the shadow of the Almighty. I will say of the Lord, 'He is my refuge and fortress; My God, in Him I will trust.' Surely He shall deliver you from the snare of the fowler And from the perilous pestilence. He shall cover you with His feathers, And under His wings you shall take refuge; His truth shall be your shield and buckler. You shall not be afraid of the terror by night, Nor of the arrow that flies by day, Nor of the pestilence that walks in darkness, Nor of the destruction that lays waste at noonday. A thousand may fall at your side, And ten thousand at your right hand; But it shall not come near you. Only with your eyes shall you look, And see the reward of the wicked. Because you have made the Lord, who is my refuge, Even the Most High, your dwelling place, No evil shall

PRAYING FOR ORGANIZATIONS, CITIES, COUNTIES, STATES, REGIONS & NATIONS | 233

befall you, Nor shall any plague come near your dwelling; For He shall give His angels charge over you, To keep you in all your ways. In their hands they shall bear you up, Lest you dash your foot against a stone. You shall tread upon the lion and the cobra, The young lion and the serpent you shall trample underfoot. 'Because he has set his love upon Me, therefore I will deliver him; I will set him on high, because he has known My name. He shall call upon Me, and I will answer him; I will be with him in trouble; I will deliver him and honor him. With long life I will satisfy him, And show him My salvation." (Psa. 91:1-16), and

Whereas, Healing is the children's bread (Mark 7:24-30, Rev. 22:2), and "By His stripes we are healed" (Isa. 53:35), and "He sent His word and healed them, And delivered them from their destructions" (Psa. 107:20), and "God anointed Jesus of Nazareth with the Holy Spirit and with power, who went about doing good and healing all who were oppressed by the devil, for God was with Him" (Acts 10:38), and

Whereas Jesus came to earth to save sinners, heal the sick, set the captives free, open the prison doors and the eyes of the blind, make the lame to walk, bring good news or glad tidings, comfort those who mourn, and proclaim the acceptable year of the Lord's favor (Isa. 61:1-3, Luke 4:18-21), and we are His hands and feet in the earth, and

Whereas, One of you can put a thousand to flight and two can rout or chase ten thousand by the hand of the Lord (Deut. 32:30), and

Whereas, Jesus said, "Again I say to you that if two of you agree on earth concerning anything that they ask, it will be done for them by My Father in heaven." (Matt. 18:19, NKJV). And we have two or more saints gathered here in agreement and unity.

## BODY:

Now therefore, we boldly and unashamedly declare the following:

Our Father, which art in heaven, Hallowed be thy Name. Thy Kingdom come. Thy will be done on earth, as it is in heaven.

We declare and proclaim this for our (city, county, state, region, nation or continent), the _____(name the geographical/ governmental area or entity you are praying for).

Father we pray Your Kingdom be established and Your will be done on earth and on the _____ , (name the geographical/governmental area or entity you are praying for) as it is in heaven.

Lord, you said, all authority in heaven and on earth has been given to You. We declare Your divine authority, bless and protection over our neighborhoods, over our families and over our properties, our health and physical bodies, our marriages, our calling, destinies and assignments, our spiritual gifts, and our assets, businesses, ministries, investments, trusts, insurance policies, bank accounts, and finances, and our alms, tithes, and offerings.

PRAYING FOR ORGANIZATIONS, CITIES, COUNTIES, STATES, REGIONS & NATIONS | 235

Your word declares, "Behold, I have set before you an open door, which no one is able to shut." We pray open doors to men's and women's hearts for salvation, truth, healing, and deliverance.

Bring them from east and west and from the north and south. Save them, set them free and fill them with your Spirit and let them be born again and made new.

We declare and proclaim: Where there is hatred, let us sow love; where there is injury, pardon; where there is discord, union; where there is doubt, faith; where there is despair, hope; where there is darkness, light; where there is sadness, joy; where there is anxiety, peace; where there is fear, courage; where is doubt and unbelief, faith; where there is insecurity, trust; where there is striving and lack of sleep, rest and sweet sleep; where there is sickness or disease, healing.

You have said in Job 22:27-28, "You will make your prayer to Him, He will hear you, And you will pay your vows. You will also declare a thing, And it will be established for you; So light will shine on your ways". We agree with Your word and with heaven, and we declare Isa. 55:11, "So shall My word be that goes forth from My mouth; It shall not return to Me void, But it shall accomplish what I please, And it shall prosper in the thing for which I sent it." Jesus said in Matt. 24:35, "Heaven and earth will pass away, but My words will by no means pass away." Psa. 119:89 says, "Your word, O LORD, is everlasting; it is firmly fixed in the heavens." And finally, Jer. 1:12 reads, "The LORD said to me, "You have seen correctly, for I am watching to see that my word is fulfilled."

## CLOSING

We declare and proclaim Your word in the midst of the assembly in Jesus' name, and in the Courts of Heaven, and seal it with the blood of Jesus, and the bond of unity and agreement of the saints. Where the brethren dwell together in unity, there the Lord commands a blessing (Psa. 133). Amen!

# CONCLUSION

As we close this last chapter, I bless you to fulfill your purpose and destiny, to complete your assignments on the earth and in heaven, to grow into the fullness and maturity of Christ, to be fruitful and multiply, and to make disciples of and in the nations.

I would enjoy hearing testimonies from you of how this book and these prayers have helped you. I invite you to email me at **brucecook77@gmail.com**. May God bless you and Godspeed.

# EPILOGUE

Thanks for taking this journey with me and welcome to the growing number of Courts of Heaven alumni. People come to the Courts from all different walks of life and backgrounds and for a wide variety of reasons. I pray that you have benefited and grown from this experience and interaction with the heavenly court system as much as I have. Now that you have been to the Courts of Heaven, faced your Accuser(s), presented your case, repented of any personal sins and sins in your ancestral bloodline, entered your plea, and received a verdict from the Supreme Judge, what will you do with your new level of relief and freedom you have received?

Most or perhaps all of you are familiar with the concept of opportunity cost, which is defined as "the loss of potential gain from other alternatives when one alternative is chosen." Many of you have experienced significant opportunity cost in the past, due to decisions you made and actions you took, which did not turn out well, or the way you were expecting or hoping for. Likewise, I believe there are also similar concepts of "identity cost," "destiny cost," and "stewardship cost" which no doubt apply to many of you as well. The cost of false identities and aborted or delayed destinies is very high—in fact, far too high. As we discussed in the last section, our God is the God who makes all things new and brings restoration.

# YOU ARE CALLED TO BE A WISE STEWARD

Luke 12:48 (CSB) says:

*"From everyone to whom much has been given, much will be required."*

So, this new level of relief and freedom you have received in the Courts of Heaven, while a free gift from God, comes with the cost of increased responsibility, and will now involve and require wise stewardship on your part. Jas. 1:17 (NIV) says:

*Every good and perfect gift is from above, coming down from the Father of the heavenly lights, who does not change like shifting shadows.*

If every gift is from our heavenly Father, then they belong to Him, and we are simply stewards, or managers, of all He has created. Among those gifts are His love, hospitality, and encouragement. 1 Pet. 4:8-10 (NKJV) says:

*And above all things have fervent love for one another, for "love will cover a multitude of sins." Be hospitable to one another without grumbling. As each one has received a gift, minister it to one another, as good stewards of the manifold grace of God.*

In verse 10 above, the Greek word for "steward" is *oikonomos*, which comes from *oikos* ("house") and *nemo* ("to arrange"). This word referred to the manager of a household or estate and later came to mean its steward. In 1 Peter 4:10, stewards use their gifts to build up and encourage others. Psa. 24:1 (NIV) says:

> The earth is the LORD's, and everything in it.

The KJV translation notes:

> The earth is the Lord's, and the fullness thereof, the world, and everything that dwells therein.

We are stewards of all God has created. We're administrators of all He gives, including what He pours into us out of His wealth and abundance.

God has blessed us with resources of time, talent, and treasure, as well as wisdom, work and wealth. He calls us to manage them with godly authority, wisdom, prudence, humility, integrity, discernment and obedience. We are responsible and effective stewards of His time when we obediently and diligently obey the commands He gives us. The fruit of the Spirit will grow best when we couple times of activity with times of rest and meditation. Our times are in God's hands (Psa. 31:15). We can trust that our earthly (*chronos*) time unfolds with ripe windows of opportune and strategic (*kairos*) times ordained in heaven. We are wise stewards when we manage our time with intentionality, while recognizing God's sovereignty and wisdom in causing

THE FRUIT OF THE SPIRIT WILL GROW BEST WHEN WE COUPLE TIMES OF ACTIVITY WITH TIMES OF REST AND MEDITATION.

or allowing events to transpire, and allowing our schedules to be interrupted by God.

God has given each of us divine gifts so that we can steward them joyfully, willingly, and wisely. He calls us to be good stewards of His mysteries. 1 Cor. 4:1-2 (NKJV) says:

> Let a man so consider us, as servants of Christ and stewards of the mysteries of God. Moreover it is required in stewards that one be found faithful.

Faithful here means integrous, honest, diligent and prudent.

A steward is not the owner, but rather the overseer or manager of resources with the best interests and practices of the owner in mind. 1 Tim. 6:7 (NIV) says:

> For we brought nothing into the world, and we can take nothing out of it.

Whatever we accumulate on earth, remains on earth, but we can store up treasure in heaven. Matt. 6:19-21 (ESV, NKJV) says:

> "Do not lay up for yourselves treasures on earth, where moth and rust destroy and where thieves break in and steal; but lay up for yourselves treasures in heaven, where neither moth nor rust destroys and where thieves do not break in and steal. For where your treasure is, there your heart will be also."

Jesus said that faithful and wise stewards are known by their obedience (Luke 12:43-44). A good steward "is faithful in what is least" and "is faithful also in much" (Luke 16:10, KJV, NKJV).

God rewards us when we invest kingdom resources—our treasures—wisely. In Matthew 25, Jesus told the Parable of the Talents. A man going on a journey entrusted his wealth to three servants. He gave each of them gold to invest or trade: one servant received five bags, one received two, and one received a single bag of gold. After a long time, the master returned and asked each what they had done with the gold they were given to manage. The servants with five bags and two bags doubled what they had been given. But, the servant with only one bag hid his gold in the ground.

In the parable, the master gave the single bag to the servant who had ten. Christ said, *"For whoever has will be given more, and they will have an abundance. Whoever does not have, even what they have will be taken from them"* (Matt. 25:29, NIV). The Lord honors our faithfulness to invest His gifts with the intent of increase. Good stewardship never buries kingdom gold, talents, treasure, or resources. When we invest wisely, a regenerative spirit and multiplication are released for the body of Christ and the larger world.

A good steward believes that the sovereign Lord is about to shift things in his or her favor. A good steward fills his or her mind and self-talk with hope from heaven about the future. *"Therefore I tell you, whatever you ask in prayer, believe that you have received it, and it will be yours"* (Mark 11:24, ESV). Doubt might temporarily distract us from Christ certainties, but Jesus is our primary focus. He is always good; sometimes, like a radar using radio waves to detect aircraft, we need to make "sweeps" for His goodness and favor. We are likely to come across His wide, long, high, and deep love along the way.

A godly steward manages Holy Spirit lenses by asking questions to gain His perspective. "Holy Spirit, what's going on? How must I shift my thinking to see what You see?" Then, with His upward lift to new elevations in the heavenly realm (Col. 3:1-2), we can reach forward and refocus or reprioritize from a whole new vantage point.

Kingdom stewards are unselfish and other-centric, keeping others in mind and looking after their needs. Phil. 2:4 (ESV) states:

> Let each of you look not only to his own interests, but also to the interests of others.

James 1:27 (BSB) adds:

> Pure and undefiled religion before our God and Father is this: to care for orphans and widows in their distress, and to keep oneself from being polluted by the world.

2 Cor. 9:8 (NIV) says:

> And God is able to make all grace abound to you, so that in all things at all times, having all that you need, you will abound in every good work.

All grace is a lot of grace, and every good work is a lot of works.

Kingdom stewards are also diligent, both in natural resources and things of the Spirit. Prov. 10:4 (ESV) says:

> A slack hand causes poverty, but the hand of the diligent makes rich.

Prov. 12:24 (ESV) adds:

EPILOGUE | 243

*The hand of the diligent will rule, while the slothful will be put to forced labor.*

Prov. 13:4 (ESV, NASB) states:

*The soul of the sluggard craves and gets nothing, But the soul of the diligent is made fat (or richly supplied).*

Prov. 21:5 (ESV) notes:

*The plans of the diligent lead surely to abundance, but everyone who is hasty comes to poverty.*

Deut. 4:9 (NASB) records:

*Only give heed to yourself and keep your soul diligently, so that you do not forget the things which your eyes have seen and they do not depart from your heart all the days of your life; but make them known to your sons and your grandsons.*

Heb. 6:11 (NASB) says:

*And we desire that each one of you show the same diligence so as to realize the full assurance of hope until the end.*

And finally, 2 Peter 3:14 (NASB) states:

*Therefore, beloved, since you look for these things, be diligent to be found by Him in peace, spotless and blameless.*

When we are stewards of Christ-possibilities, we see that God redeems our past and releases expansive, explosive possibilities for our futures. As Jesus has redeemed us from sin, even so we are to redeem our time on earth and use it to full advantage. And, it's never too late with God on our side. You are right on time and were born in the fullness of time for the destiny and purpose for which you were created by God. Use your new level of freedom to do the greater works Jesus mentioned in John 14:12, and to do mighty exploits or deeds (Dan. 11:32) as one who knows their God. Change the world one day and one person at a time for Christ.

CHANGE THE WORLD ONE DAY AND ONE
PERSON AT A TIME FOR CHRIST.

# APPENDIX A
# QUESTIONS AND ANSWERS

I thought it would be helpful to list and answer some commonly-asked questions here at the end.

1. CAN A PERSON WHO IS NOT A CHRISTIAN ACCESS AND/OR PARTICIPATE IN THE COURTS OF HEAVEN?
   No. I believe it is necessary that you have a saving relationship with Jesus in order to access the Courts of Heaven. Otherwise, Jesus would not be your Advocate to defend you and the blood of Jesus would not be speaking on your behalf, your sins would not be forgiven, you would not be born again and adopted into the family of God, and the Holy Spirit would not be living inside of you to help guide you, comfort you, teach you, bring things to your remembrance, and lead you into all truth. However, salvation is available to all who believe and call on the name of Jesus and confess and repent of their sins.

For unbelievers, their sins would still be separating them from God. This right to appear in the Courts of Heaven is called standing, which is a legal term, and all saints have this right because of the blood of Jesus, His righteousness and finished work on the cross, His ongoing work in heaven, and our relationship to Him as a new creation and as joint heirs who have been adopted into the family of God.

2.  CAN A HUSBAND AND WIFE HAVE A JOINT SESSION IN THE COURTS OF HEAVEN?

Yes, I have found this works very well as long as both parties are Christians and trust each other, and the parties can either read the prayers of repentance for each chapter together in unison, or read them separately, one at a time, as they prefer. Most couples read the prayers together in unison. Keep in mind that each party has its own bloodline, since each spouse has different parents.

If one or both spouses have secret sins that they are ashamed of, and have not shared with each other, then they may prefer to have a private session by themselves.

3.  CAN MULTIPLE SIBLINGS BE PART OF THE SAME SESSION IN THE COURTS OF HEAVEN?

Yes. It helps if they each have the same father and mother, but it is still possible otherwise, although there would be more bloodlines represented in that case. There are many blended families and adopted families—lots of step-brothers, step-sisters, half-brothers, half-sisters, those who are the biological children of parents, and those who are the adopted children of parents. The parties can either read the prayers of repentance for each chapter together in unison, or read them separately, one at a time, as they prefer.

QUESTIONS AND ANSWERS | 247

4. CAN A HUSBAND AND WIFE AND THEIR CHILDREN HAVE A JOINT SESSION IN THE COURTS OF HEAVEN?

Yes, although in practical terms, the parents may prefer to have some privacy or confidentiality in regard to the sin issues in their ancestral bloodlines and in their own lives. Moreover, the children would have to be old enough to understand right and wrong and be aware of sin, and to have made a salvation decision for themselves by accepting Jesus as their Lord and Savior and repenting of and confessing their sins, and their faith in Christ.

Oftentimes, older children also prefer their privacy and confidentiality in repenting of sins. However, I have led a few such sessions with parents and one or more teen-aged children involved. These are usually special situations involving such issues as suicide, an unwanted pregnancy, serious health issue, etc. But, there are some families that are strong enough and where there is a high degree of love, support, trust, and transparency with each other, who would do well with a family session.

5. ISN'T THE BLOOD OF JESUS ENOUGH?

Yes, the blood of Jesus is enough to cover your sins and the sins of all who believe on Him and call upon His name. But, most, if not all, people have unsaved relatives and forefathers in their ancestral bloodlines who sinned and did not know Jesus, and therefore did not confess and repent of their sins, and were not saved. They may also have made covenants, oaths or vows which involved generational curses. These are open issues that Satan can legally use against you and your family through your ancestral bloodline.

## 6. CAN A PERSON STAND IN PROXY FOR THEIR UNSAVED OR BACKSLIDDEN RELATIVE(S) IN THE COURTS OF HEAVEN?

Yes. Most often this question comes from parents who want to pray for their prodigal children in the Courts of Heaven. My team and I have led sessions like this on several occasions with one or both parents standing in proxy for their unbelieving or backslidden child or children. I am well aware there are many one-parent homes also, and God bless those heroes who raise children without a spouse. The faith of the believing parent can touch God's heart and can potentially benefit their child or children as they do the repentance work for their ancestral bloodline. The child receives an indirect benefit of this since they are part of the same bloodline.

Of course, if both parents participate, it is even more helpful since both sides of the bloodline get cleansed. Please note: I am NOT saying that believing parents can remit or absolve the sins of their unbelieving, unrepentant or backslidden prodigal child or children, except for the sins toward them personally, according to John 20:23. Both Jesus and Stephen the martyr modeled that type of forgiveness and remission of sins toward those who killed them and accused them falsely. And, we can do the same for those who mistreat or persecute and sin against us. But, only Jesus, the Savior of mankind, can forgive the sins of the whole world. Other applications of this would be for believing siblings to pray for their unbelieving or backslidden siblings in proxy, or for a believing spouse to pray for their unbelieving or backslidden marriage partner in proxy.

# APPENDIX B
# DECLARATIONS AND DECREES OF REPENTANCE

I make these declarations for myself, for my ancestral bloodline, and for all of those who are joined to us by covenant or contract. In the declarations below, the word "We" is used repeatedly and represents and stands for all three of these groups.

> I request that Jesus, my Advocate, Mediator, and High Priest, represent me before this Court. I also invite and authorize this Courts of Heaven team to help represent me in this Court and assist in these legal proceedings. I ask that my Counselor, Holy Spirit, obtain and produce before this Court all of Heaven's records, as well as records held by the kingdom of darkness, and any earthly courts, governments, agencies or institutions. I call for all entries that are contained in these records to be revealed that affect me, my bloodline, and those joined to me by

covenant or contract. By faith according to Psalm 139, I request the book of my purpose, identity and destiny to be released to me fully today. I further request that any and all seals on my book be broken and the full contents be released and opened today. I further request that the members of this ministry team be granted words of knowledge, words of wisdom, discerning of spirits, revelation and prophetic visions and utterance to recognize, understand, read, interpret, describe and declare, or otherwise express, entries in Heaven's records.

I ask that my heart, mind, imagination and spirit be acutely aware of each matter brought before the Court.

I now call for the Records of Heaven to be presented to expose each and every lie and grounds for accusations that have been thought, imagined, spoken by or agreed with by me and all members of my ancestral bloodline and those joined to us by covenant.

## SELF:

We forgive ourselves for all disappointed results, false judgments, character shortcomings, sins, iniquities, transgressions, fears and failure to act when we had the opportunity to do so.

We choose to accept and confess that we are not perfect, and we forgive ourselves!

We repent of each act, thought and word by which we have sinned against others in these same ways.

## MINISTERS:

We thank you for the ministers and spiritual leaders you have sent to us to teach and train us and watch over our souls, and for those who have sown spiritually into our lives by word, deed, and example, and we bless and honor them now and pray for them and their families for wisdom and health and safety and protection and provision and encouragement and strength and refreshing, and we ask you Lord to also bless and honor them and promote them in your service. We forgive all human ministers, church leaders (pastors, teachers, priests, bishops, apostles, prophets, evangelists, missionaries, elders, deacons, etc.), and fellow Christians who have ever failed, disappointed, offended or wounded us and not fully or perfectly reflected or modeled Christ Jesus.

We forgive them for any and all failures, weaknesses, sins and shortcomings that affected us, including permitting and/or committing abuse, deception, intimidation, neglect, betrayal, false judgments, false teaching, dishonor, favoritism, organizational politics or a political spirit, gossip, slander, coercion and manipulation, lack of love, lack of wisdom, lack of discernment, lack of diplomacy and tact, lack of gentleness and kindness, lack of sensitivity, in the performance of their duties, or the execution of their offices, as those delegated with divine and legal authority.

We also repent of each act, thought and word by which we have sinned against others in these same ways, and we forgive ourselves.

## OTHER PEOPLE:

We forgive all other humans for theft, extortion, deception, abuse in any form, failure to bless, withholding opportunity, perversion of justice, instilling fear, participation in and teaching of false religion, idolatry, and the occult. We repent of any and all broken contracts, covenants, promises, oaths, vows, acts of violence, alliances, associations, or pacts that have been formed willingly or unwillingly.

We also repent of each act, thought and word by which we have sinned against others in these same ways.

## CURSES:

We renounce and break agreement with every curse and false judgment spoken over us, or released against us. We repent of and break each curse and false judgment spoken unrighteously by us over others and/or over ourselves.

## REPLACEMENT OF LIES WITH TRUTH:

We now repent of each and every lie and falsehood, and renounce them all.

We ask that Jesus, our Advocate, apply His blood to blot out each lie in Heaven's records.

Now, we invite Father who is true, Jesus who is the truth, and the Holy Spirit of Truth, to speak Truth to each of us, and write the Truth of our Divine identity and destiny upon our hearts, minds, imagination, and lips.

## UNRIGHTEOUS LENSES AND FILTERS:

We repent of and renounce any and all unhealthy and/or unrighteous lenses, filters, triggers, trigger mechanisms, hot buttons, flash points, walls, fortresses, strongholds, footholds, and defense mechanisms, and we cut ties to them and break agreement with them now, in Jesus name. We invite and beseech you, Lord, to disarm them, deactivate them, decommission them, dismantle them, and destroy them now. In the mighty name of Jesus, Amen!

## THE POWER OF ADDICTIONS:

We break agreement with and renounce all destructive addictions in every form. We repent and ask for forgiveness for agreeing with and acting out of a spirit of powerlessness, discouragement, self-pity, hopelessness, passive aggressive behaviors, co-dependence, victimhood and blame shifting. From this day forward, we ask you Lord to set us free from the controlling influences of all addictive substances, behaviors and thoughts. We ask you Lord to set us free from all compulsive and obsessive thoughts and actions. In the mighty name of Jesus, Amen.

"I WILL GRACIOUSLY GIVE YOU A NEW, TENDER HEART AND PUT A NEW, WILLING SPIRIT INSIDE YOU. I WILL REMOVE YOUR HARD HEART OF STONE AND GIVE YOU AN OBEDIENT, RESPONSIVE HEART INSTEAD. I WILL PUT MY HOLY SPIRIT IN YOU AND EMPOWER YOU TO KEEP MY LAWS AND TO LIVE BY THEM."

– EZEKIEL 36:25-27 (TPT)